MORE THAN THE GIFT

More Than Stewardship
More Than Rewards

A LOVE RELATIONSHIP

Larry J. Robinson

COPYRIGHTS
© 2009, Larry Robinson
First Edition
All Rights Reserved.

This material may not be reproduced in any form without the prior written permission of the author (subject to fair usage guidelines). All inquiries should be forwarded to the author at morethanthegift@comcast.net.

Scripture taken from the HOLY BIBLE: NEW INTERNATIONAL VERSION®. NIV®. Copyright © 1973, 1978, 1984 by International Bible Society. Used by permission of Zondervan

Scripture quotations marked "TNIV" are taken from the Holy Bible, Today's New International Version™ TNIV® Copyright© 2001, 2005 by International Bible Society® Used by permission under fair usage guidelines. All rights reserved worldwide.

Scripture quotations marked "NKJV" are taken from the New King James Version®. Copyright © 1982 by Thomas Nelson, Inc. Used by permission under fair usage guidelines. All rights reserved.

Italics have been added by the author for emphasis.
Cover design: Eddy Gordon

ISBN: 1-59330-594-X
Library of Congress Control Number: 2009930804
Library of Congress Cataloging-in-Publication Data

ACKNOWLEDGMENTS

I thank and praise God for His grace in continuing to provide opportunities for me to convey this message.

I thank Sharon (still my muse, still my missing rib, still my wife, still my life) for her continued support and unfailing love.

I thank my mother-in-law, Nancy, and my sisters Johnnie, Gladys and Valerie for believing in the vision from the beginning and being consistent with their encouragement.

I thank my sons (Torian, Nathan, Julian and Garrett) who serve as God's messengers, revealing unto me spiritual truths that I draw upon in my writing, teaching and living.

I thank each of the church families who have helped nurture my relationship with the Lord: Union Hill MB Church (Chicago, Illinois), United MB Church (Chicago, Illinois), St. Paul AME Church (Cambridge, Massachusetts) and Second Baptist Church of Wheaton (Wheaton, Illinois).

I am blessed!

Table Of Contents

Acknowledgments	3
Preface	6
Providing Context	7
God Is Interested in More Than Just Our Gift	21
God's Interest in the Giver	23
God's Interest in the Giver's Willingness	27
God's Interest in the Giver's Relationship with Him	32
God's Interest in the Giver's Relationship with Others	37
God's Interest in More than the Giver's Hand	42
God's Interest in the Giver's Faith	46
The Gift Is Still Important Because of What It Reveals	51
Our Giving Reveals the Giver's Love	53
Our Giving Reveals the Giver's Gratitude	58
Our Giving Reveals the Giver's Understanding of God's Ownership	63
Our Giving Reveals the Giver's Stewardship	69
Our Giving Reveals the Giver's Reverence	75
Our Giving Reveals the Giver's Treasure and Heart	81

THE GIFT IS STILL IMPORTANT BECAUSE OF WHAT IT ACCOMPLISHES	85
WHAT OUR GIVING ACCOMPLISHES: GOD'S PROVISION FOR HIS MINISTRY	87
WHAT OUR GIVING ACCOMPLISHES: OUR FELLOWSHIP IN MINISTRY	92
WHAT OUR GIVING ACCOMPLISHES: POSITIONS US FOR GREATER BLESSING	98
WHAT OUR GIVING ACCOMPLISHES: OUR PREPARATION FOR ETERNITY	103
WHAT OUR GIVING ACCOMPLISHES: OUR PREPARATION FOR OUR INHERITANCE	110
WHAT OUR GIVING ACCOMPLISHES: BRINGING GLORY TO GOD	117
NOTES	124

Preface

During the past few years, I have felt led to help broaden the conversations within the Christian community regarding our giving. My reflections in this book are intended to inspire readers to reexamine their perspective on giving by guiding the reader's focus toward God and His purposes in the process. At the center of God's purposes are His love for us and our response to that love. I pray that by reflecting on our giving in the context of our love relationship with our Father, readers will discover the breadth of meaning and purpose that God embeds in the gift of giving He bestows upon us. Our giving always has been and continues to be about so much more than the gift itself.

For a Bible study on this subject, please refer to *More Than The Gift – The Workbook*. To discover more about this project and the additional resources that are available for your inspiration, education and use, please visit my website: morethanthegift.net, my blogsite: christiangiving.blogspot.com and my podcasts on the iTunes Store.

Providing Context

There are aspects of the biblical treatment of the topic of giving that many Christians find puzzling or uncomfortable. This is especially true of the relationship between our offertory giving and our spiritual health. For many of us, that relationship neither makes sense to us nor fits comfortably with how we want to conduct our lives. In Luke 3:7–11, John was baptizing in the Jordan River, preaching about the forgiveness of sins and warning the crowd that their lack of spiritual fruitfulness made them vulnerable to the coming day of reckoning. The crowd cried out to John, "What should we do then?" John's answer? Share what you have with someone who has less than you.

Was John ministering or was he meddling? No one had asked John about how to conduct his or her financial affairs. They were asking about forgiveness, about repentance, about salvation from the penalty of their spiritual barrenness, but John's first response was about giving. Had John gotten off message? After all, John was only a messenger, not the messiah.

In Mark 10:17–22 we find a similar passage involving Jesus. A young man asks the question: "What must I do to obtain eternal life?" Jesus challenged him to sell everything he owned and give the proceeds to the poor. The young man's response was to turn and walk away. Why did Jesus ask the man to give so much? Is that what Jesus requires of everyone, including us? For some of us, such passages are puzzling. For some of us, they are uncomfortable.

Maybe it is the fear that people will turn and walk away that has constrained ministers and teachers in today's churches in helping the people of God solve their sense of puzzlement or get past their discomfort. It's not that church leaders don't ask people to give; it's just that we haven't been very effective in helping people discern God's intent. While some might walk away, I am convinced that for many of us the true problem is our lack of understanding of what God is really asking of us. We understand the words of scripture, but not their true meaning or connection to each other. For many, a clearer understanding of God's purposes for our giving would be both exciting and inviting, but people are suffering from a lack of knowledge. While, it is not always given to us to know God's purposes and plans, there are times He chooses to reveal to us what can be known. I believe that now is such a time.

Each week, tens of millions of Christians throughout the world give offerings during the worship services they attend. Each week, millions of us give without considering the reasons why God has asked us to give and what purposes He has in mind. Each week, many of us give offerings with which God is not pleased without understanding the reasons for His displeasure. Each week, ritual precedes relationship in the giving of too many of us. Yet in his book, *Money Possessions & Eternity,* Christian author Randy Alcorn reports that only 1–2 percent of Christian colleges have classes on biblical financial principles and stewardship, only 2–4 percent of seminaries offer such courses, only 15 percent of pastors say that they have been equipped by either their denomination or seminary to handle the topic and that only 10 percent of churches have active programs to teach these principles to their congregants.[1]

Maybe church leaders are also afraid that if we place too much emphasis on the topic of giving, we will offend our church members or seem too carnally minded. Whatever the reason, many ministers and teachers minimize their teaching regarding the topic. The reluctance to teach biblical offertory principles negatively impacts not only those who are puzzled or uncomfortable, but also those who simply have not been exposed to substantive teaching regarding God's purposes and plans for our giving. Each group is denied the benefit of exposure to the broad counsel of God contained in the scriptures regarding this topic. This inadequately prepares our church members to recognize the errant teachings they may encounter or to actively pursue and experience the breadth of God's purposes for their giving.

It has been estimated that the scriptures contain three times more verses on our handling of material possessions (or treasure) than verses on love, seven times more on our material possessions than prayer and eight times more on our material treasure than belief. It has been calculated that 15 percent of the verses in the Bible deal with the subject of material possessions.[2] Based on the sheer volume of scripture devoted to the subject, it is undeniable that God considers your stewardship of material treasure of the utmost importance. This is not a fabrication of the preacher. It is not a plot of manipulation by the trustees or finance committee. It is the word of God.

However, it is possible to grasp the significance of a biblical principle yet still misunderstand the reason why the principle is emphasized. It is clear to me that while some of us have grasped the importance of the principle of giving; many of us still fail to see what God is accomplishing through the process. So when church leaders talk about giving without adequately teaching about God's intent, people in the pews can be left confused about the place of money in God's value system. Given an inaccurate understanding of the true focus of God's attention, leaders and church members alike tend to get bent out of shape over money. Members leave. Pastors, deacons and trustees argue. Churches split. People "lose their religion" over money. However, I would suggest that we step back and ask ourselves whether we really believe that the emphasis of the scriptures is truly about money or material possessions. I think we need to remind ourselves that Christ did not suffer, bleed or die for "dollar bills." The great commission is not a call to go forth and raise funds, but a call to go forth and raise disciples. The great commission is a call for kingdom building. Our treatment of our treasure has a place in the building plan, but it is never the actual focus of God's plan.

For many of us (like the rich young ruler whom Jesus encounters in Luke), our discomfort revolves around the issue of the magnitude of our giving. We are willing to give—but struggle with giving sacrificially. However, from God's perspective the problem goes much deeper than an issue of the content of our gift. God is forever focused on the heart with which we give. My son Garrett recently gave me a glimpse of a giver's heart.

It was my birthday. The family and I were sitting in the family room and I was preparing to open the gifts they had given. Garrett is my youngest son and he was five years old at the time. He was very excited and full of anticipation. As I began to unwrap a present, he ran to me and asked, "Dad, would you open mine first?" How could I refuse? Opening his gift, I discovered that he had given a battery-powered Gillette razor. Bursting with joy, he explained, "Dad, you need this. This razor has five blades and your old razor only has four." Then he added a surprising request: "Dad, can I watch you use it?" I thanked

Garrett for his gift and explained that it was evening and that I usually shaved early in the morning. He could watch me then. Garrett was the first one to awaken the next morning. Running to my bedside, he again requested, "Dad, can I watch you use it?" I immediately arose, lathered up my face and began to shave. As he watched with sparkling eyes, Garrett had never seemed happier or more fulfilled.

Can you imagine what our churches would be like if each member gave of their time, their talent and their treasure willingly with a joyful spirit? What it would be like if our main concern was that our gift pleased our Lord and brought benefit to the kingdom? What would it be like if we came unto the Lord saying: "I know there is a need somewhere in the kingdom, I don't have much to give, but I know that if I put it in Your hands it can make a difference. All that I have has come from You and I'm willing to give back to You from what You have given me. I thank You for the opportunity to give and all I ask is that it be used according to Your will. Use it to bless the work of ministry. Use it to bless the workers of ministry. Use it so that Your kingdom comes. Use it that Your will be done. Use it to glorify Your Name."

Too often a heart of worship seems missing from our giving. Christians give, but many give under the burden of obligation or for self-serving reasons. We give, but remain puzzled, uncomfortable and/or uninformed. Something needs to change, but let me suggest that if we continue to teach principles of giving in the same way we always have, it is very likely that we will get the same result we've always gotten. Something needs to change. So I believe that God is revealing a word of clarity for what confuses His people, a word of comfort for what troubles them, a timely message from the depths of His timeless word to inform His people.

Through the More Than The Gift ministry, I believe He is calling me to help expand what we think, what we speak, what we teach, what we preach and what we practice regarding our giving to the Lord. You see, this week need not be like every other week because God is inviting us to deepen our understanding of His purposes and plans for our giving.

The truth of the matter is that God is up to something special through the process of our giving. God wants His children to see the connection between His messages in scripture regarding our giving so that His purposes would become clearer and be fulfilled. The lessons in scripture are not simply separate and distinct messages. No, they are related to each other. It's like a draw-by-number puzzle given to children in restaurants. In order for the picture to be revealed, the child needs to connect the dots. Likewise, in order for us to see what God is revealing (in order for us to get the message), it is time for the contemporary church to stop cherry-picking isolated scriptures about giving to suit our purposes and finally begin to connect the dots to discover God's purposes. I believe that He wants us to see that our giving is a tool, a path, training-wheels of His higher purposes.

A human illustration of what God is doing can be found in how parents involve their children in gift giving at an early age. Typically, a young child lacks the inclination to give. They must be taught. They also lack the resources to give. The resources must be given. When a child gives a gift to a family member, the family does not gain financially from the child's gift because the resources initially came from the family and are simply being returned to the family in another form. The goal of the process isn't the gift itself, but rather the lessons that the child learns. The lessons are about relationships. They are about love, honor, gratitude and respect. On the surface it appears that the child is the giver, but in reality the child is the receiver.

Psalms 24:1 reminds us that the earth and everything in it is the Lord's. God does not ask for our gifts that He might add to His wealth. First, He gives of His wealth to us. Then He creates opportunities for us to give back to Him. We give to Him not out of substance we actually own, but of substance we have received. We receive, then give, but in doing so we receive the greater gift. This is done for our benefit. He is teaching us the same types of lessons we try to teach our children. He is teaching about relationships that we might draw closer to Him and each other. On the surface it appears that we are the giver, but in reality we are the receiver.

Two themes seem prevalent in contemporary discussions about giving: stewardship (discussed as our duty and obligation) and rewards. Let me humbly state my position regarding each. I believe that both themes are biblical. However, I believe that neither discussion alone is sufficient to achieve God's intended purpose. God has a higher purpose for our giving than our stewardship. God also has a higher purpose for our giving than the material blessings that it triggers.

Imagine for a moment that you are walking by the room of your two children and you overhear them talking. The first child says, "Well, it's Dad's birthday again. I guess I have to buy him a gift."

"Don't you want to buy him a gift?" the other child asks.

"No, but I have to buy one," says the first child.

"What do you mean by have to?" asks the other child.

"Well, if I don't buy a gift, Dad will be sad, Mom will be angry, and you will give me grief. It's just not worth the hassle. So, I have to buy a gift."

Let me suggest that any parent hearing those words would be heartbroken. However, what if the second child continued the conversation by saying, "Well, I don't know what your problem is, but I'm going to buy Dad a good gift. You see, I've discovered that when I give Dad a five-dollar gift on his birthday he gives me a fifty-dollar gift on my birthday, and when I give him a ten-dollar gift on his birthday, he gives me a hundred-dollar gift on mine. So, I've been saving up to give him a great gift."

"Is that the only reason you give him a gift?" asks the first child.

"Sure, why else would you give a gift," the second child replies.

Let me suggest that the parent would still be heartbroken. Neither a motivation of obligation alone nor a motivation of rewards alone achieves fulfillment for both the giver and receiver. God is inviting us to view our giving in the context of our relationship with Him. It is on this foundation that all other aspects of our giving achieve their proper balance and meaning. In the context of the relationship, we begin to understand that our stewardship is not a goal, but rather a role in the relationship. Our stewardship prepares us to receive eternal inheritance. It prepares us for ownership. In the context of the relationship, we discover that rewards and blessings are not the reason to give, but are parts of the natural flow within healthy relationships with the Lord. To God, the relationship is of utmost importance. Jesus came to reconcile our broken relationship with God. Once we have been reconciled, our giving is intended to nourish and nurture our relationship with the Lord and each other.

Three central principles have emerged from what God has revealed to me thus far and form the foundation for my reflections in this book. The principles unveil the interrelated purposes and plans God has for our giving:

First Principle: God is interested in more than just the gift.

God's priority is our relationship with Him and each other. He desires to use our giving as a tool to grow those relationships. So, He repeatedly places the topic of giving in scripture next to His discussion of relationship issues that we might see the connection. It's not that the gift is not important, but the gift alone is never God's focus.

Second Principle: Our giving is important because of what it reveals.

Even though God is interested in more than our gift, our giving is important because our response to the opportunity to give serves as a mirror that reflects the health of our relationship with God.

Third Principle: Our giving is important because of what it accomplishes.
Even though God is interested in more than our gift, our giving is important because God uses it to fulfill His purposes for our relationship with Him and each other and thereby bring glory to His name.

The lessons that follow offer both practical and scriptural illustrations of these principles and reveal how God is leading me to "connect the dots" regarding the Father's purposes for our giving. My reflections are not an exhaustive discussion of the principles, but are intended to initiate a conversation within the Christian community that prayerfully will deepen our understanding of God's will for our giving and begin to positively change our perspective regarding His purposes and plans. I do not believe that it is His will that our giving continue to be guided by either misinformation or inadequate information regarding His intent. Let me conclude this section by sharing three things that I believe can result from viewing our giving through the perspective of our relationship with the Lord:

Elevated Motivations
Considering what our giving means in the context of our relationship can help inspire giving that looks beyond its immediate impact on the giver and seeks to fulfill God's desire to nurture our relationship with Him and each other. I believe that God wants to develop within us higher motivations for our giving

than the compulsion of obligation or the pursuit of our self-interest.

Rejuvenated Attitudes
Examining our giving through the lens of our relationship can help inspire giving that reflects the emotions of a healthy love relationship with our Lord. Indeed, exemplary giving in scripture often flows from the passion of the giver. God still loves a cheerful giver.

Yielded Methods
Yielding our giving to scriptural guidance can help inspire giving that is responsive both to God's Lordship and the purposes He desires to accomplish for and through His relationship with us.

When we give with motives, attitudes and methods that are yielded to the Lord, our relationship with Him is deepened and He is glorified. I pray that God blesses your moments of meditation and reflection regarding what He has shared with me and that you are inspired to share with others what He reveals to you during those moments of devotion.

God Is Interested in More Than Just Our Gift

For I desire mercy, and not sacrifice, and the knowledge of God more than burnt offerings.
— Hosea 6:6 (NKJV)

God's Interest in ---- the Giver

Food for Thought
God rejected Cain's offering. Cain responded with anger and depression. What amazes me about God's counsel to Cain is found in what God did not say. God did not say anything specifically about Cain's offering? There was something much more important at stake.

Reference Scripture
Genesis 4:3–16

Connecting the Dots:
What God has allowed me to see
Christian commentary on the reference scripture often focuses on the inappropriateness of Cain's offering, but I believe that the text is also pointing to a deeper issue. Notice in verse 4 that God looked on both the gift and the giver. God's comment to Cain was that if Cain did what was right, Cain would be accepted. The wording suggests that Cain knew what was right and had the power to do so. God desired to accept Cain, not just his offering. Finally, God also advised Cain that a choice not to do what was right was a

choice to turn from God toward sin. God warned that sin was waiting to consume Cain.

I suspect that this passage's emphasis on the giver more so than the gift often goes unnoticed by readers. Yet, this passage of scripture actually says very little about the offering itself. God focused on Cain and how Cain was relating to Him. It would have been very easy for God to have identified for us the aspect of Cain's offering that made it unacceptable. I believe that God intentionally omitted specific comments about Cain's giving in order to point us in another direction.

For me, there is a familiarity to God's approach to this Father-son chat. I often find myself trying to give general advice to my oldest son without telling him specifically what he should do. My oldest son is in his mid-twenties and is branch manager for a major financial institution in New York. Recently, he called and stated that he wanted my advice regarding a dilemma he faced at work. After listening patiently to his problem, I became convinced that he knew the correct course of action, but that course was not his preference. I was anxious because his decision would impact his career, but I also knew that it was important for my son to decide for himself, so after asking a few general questions about the situation, I said, "I can understand your dilemma, call me back and let me know what you decide." As his father, I wanted my son to make the correct decision, but I also wanted it to be the result of his self-reflection and free will.

God's comments to Cain were directed at the relationship. Cain's gift had no value outside of the context of their relationship. I believe God focused on Cain rather than the offering itself because the offering was only symptomatic of a deeper issue. God talked to Cain about Cain and not about the gift because their relationship mattered more than the gift. God did not offer specific instructions regarding how to amend the offering. Cain knew what was right in God's sight, but Cain had to choose for himself. Cain's choice needed to be the result of self-reflection and free will.

The consequences of Cain's actions are summarized in his own words in Genesis 4:13 and 14:

Genesis 4:

Ge 4:13 Cain said to the LORD, "My punishment is more than I can bear.
Ge 4:14 Today you are driving me from the land, and *I will be hidden from your presence....*"

Cain finally realized that his choices and actions bore a cost to His relationship with the Lord, yet even then he still did not realize how much that relationship mattered to God. While their initial conversation suggested the priority that God placed on Cain, God's subsequent actions reveal His heart as a father. Verses 15 and 16 reveal that after God's pronouncement of His judgment on Cain for his murder of Abel, Cain feared that someone would kill him. Yet, in spite of Cain's unacceptable offering and in spite of his murder of his brother, God chose not to abandon Cain to the judgment of his peers. God placed a mark on Cain, identifying Cain as His own and God declared that anyone who killed Cain would be punished "seven times over." So Cain remained not just under the authority of God, but under God's protection as well, even though "Cain went from the presence of the Lord" (verse 16). Wow! In spite of the breach in their relationship, God chose to continue His public identification with Cain and to extend His protection as a father.

This, the Bible's first account of mankind's offertory giving, clearly establishes God's interest in the giver and makes it easier to see that God is interested in more than just the gift.

God's Interest in
————
The Giver's Willingness

Food for Thought

Abraham had waited 25 years for the fulfillment of God's promise and then (when Abraham was 100 years old) the fulfillment came. Sarah bore her only child, Abraham's son, Abraham's heir. Isaac was a source of great joy and hope for Abraham. Isaac was a symbol of God's faithfulness and promises of blessing. So, I can't imagine the thoughts Abraham had and emotions he felt when God requested that he offer Isaac's life as a burnt offering. In spite of what he may have felt, Abraham's response was amazing. Abraham exhibited no hesitancy. He did not question, barter or argue with God. He arose early the next morning and began his journey to the appointed place of sacrifice. Abraham exhibited great faith. On the third day, Abraham instructed his servants to stay with the donkeys while he and Isaac journeyed to the appointed place of worship. Before leaving them, Abraham spoke words of faith, stating that both he and Isaac would return to them. The writer of Hebrews explains that Abraham was convinced that even if he sacrificed Isaac unto the Lord, God could raise Isaac from the dead. Abraham prepared to offer Isaac's life not knowing that Isaac's life was not the offering that God was really seeking. At the appointed time, God provided Abraham with a substitute object of sacrifice, a ram in the bush. Why was a substitute acceptable? Why was a sacrifice of lesser value sufficient? It was acceptable because, more than the tangible object of Abraham's giving, the offering God was seeking was Abraham's willingness to withhold nothing from Him. In raising the knife of sacrifice to offer his son, Abraham demonstrated to himself and us his unrestrained willingness to give his all to the Lord. No object of sacrifice was greater than the gift he had already given.

Reference Scriptures
  2 Corinthians 9:7
  1 Chronicles 29:3–17
  2 Corinthians 8:3–12

Connecting the Dots:
What God has allowed me to see

Much of Christian discussion about offertory giving seems to focus on the content of the gift, but the Holy Scriptures make it very clear that the acceptability of our gifts depends on much more than their content. Paul's instruction in 2 Corinthians 9:7 summarizes (as a general principle) the appeal Paul had made to the Corinthians regarding their gift to help the believers in Jerusalem. In anticipation of their gift, Paul had boasted about their generosity and urged that they collect their offering in advance so that it reflected their willing generosity rather than appearing to be a gift that was given grudgingly. The reference verse establishes a fundamental criterion for the acceptability of our gifts. It establishes the need for a personal decision in our giving that is neither reluctant nor under compulsion. God desires our willingness and He loves a cheerful giver.

David and Israel's leaders demonstrated this type of attitude when they gave an offering to finance the building of the temple. Three elements from the account in 1 Chronicles 29 seem relevant to our discussion. First, there is a subtle, but key message in the appeal David made prior to Israel's leaders giving their offering. Rather than just asking them to give an offering, David asked who was willing to consecrate themselves to the Lord. It is clear that David understood that God desires more than the substance of our gifts. Our willingness involves more than things. It involves us. The second element involves the people's response to the offering given by their leaders. The leaders responded to David's appeal by giving an offering that would be worth more than a billion dollars today. The amount given was mind boggling, yet the scripture says that the people rejoiced that the leaders had given willingly and with their whole heart. The people focused on *how* the leaders gave rather than solely on *what* they gave. This is God's focus also. The third element is found in David's prayer of thanks to God. In it, David comments that God uses our giving to test us. In response to their test, David notes that he and Israel had given willingly and honestly. Embedded in this prayer is David's message to us that one of the reasons God presents to us opportunities to give is to test our willingness to do so.

In 2 Corinthians 8:5 Paul shares how the Macedonian Christians had approached their giving in the same manner as David and the Israelite leaders. Like the Israelites, the Macedonians first gave themselves to the Lord. Paul then uses the approach of the Macedonians to illustrate what that really means. Rather than exercising their own wills in their giving, they submitted themselves to the will of God. It was their submission to God's will that empowered them to give beyond Paul's expectation, even though they were impoverished. Verses 3 and 4 expand on the effect of their submission to God's will. Paul notes that the Macedonians pleaded with him for the privilege to give and had given above their apparent ability of their own accord.

Finally, verse 12 provides a synthesis of the principles we have discussed. Paul writes, "For if the willingness is there, the gift is acceptable according to what one has, not according to what one does not have." This passage makes it clear that God desires to move our focus beyond just the gift itself. The magnitude of our gift is not of critical importance. David and the Israelite leaders gave out of their wealth, while the Macedonian Christians gave out of their poverty. In each instance, their giving was marked by their willingness. It was their offering of willingness that guided the substance of their giving and pleased God. As verse 12 reminds us, only if there is willingness can our gifts find favor with God.

God's Interest in
————
the Giver's Relationship with Him

Food for Thought

"One of them, an expert in the law, tested him with this question. Teacher, which is the greatest commandment in the Law? Jesus replied, *Love the Lord your God with all your heart and with all your soul and with all your mind. This is the first and greatest commandment*" (Matthew 22:35–38). In this response to a question from the crowd, Jesus establishes that our highest pursuit is our love relationship with the Father. All other requirements flow from the pursuit of that relationship, even our giving.

Reference Scriptures
Malachi 3:6–8
Hosea 6:6
John 17:3

Connecting the Dots:
What God has allowed me to see

The verses that follow the reference scripture from Malachi are often quoted during offertory appeals and set forth one of the great challenges in scripture regarding our offertory giving.

Verses 10–12 read:

"Bring the whole tithe into the storehouse that there may be food in my house. Test me in this," says the Lord Almighty, *"and see if I will not throw open the floodgates of heaven and pour out so much blessing that there will not be room enough to store it. I will prevent pests from devouring your crops and the vines in your fields will not drop their fruit before it is ripe,"* says the Lord Almighty. *"Then all the nations will call you blessed, for yours will be a delightful land,"* says the Lord Almighty.

These verses are full of promise and God openly asks the reader to test Him through their giving. These verses remain lodged in my memory from my earliest years as a Christian youth. They helped shape my giving practices while I was still an adolescent.

Yet, as wonderful as this portion of the passage is, I believe that it is only in the context of the preceding verses that we learn the true focus of both the challenge and the promise. God's focus is not simply to secure food for His house. Nor is His primary intent to remove the curse being experienced by His wayward children and replace it with blessings. These are the natural consequence for the challenge, but not the reason. What the preceding verses reveal is that Israel had consistently breached its covenant relationship with the Lord by their disobedience. The focus of this passage is on that relationship.

The phrase that strikes me most profoundly from the reference verses is this:

"Return to me, and I will return to you," says the Lord of hosts. "But you said, 'In what way shall we return?'"

In this passage, God is seeking to restore His relationship with His chosen people. They have repeatedly strayed away from their fellowship with Him. The earlier chapters and verses speak to their dishonoring attitudes toward giving, the corruption of their priests, the practice of sorcery, their infidelity in marriage, and their injustice toward others. God promised to send His messenger who would purge His people of these practices so that they could present to the Lord offerings of righteousness, offerings that would be pleasant unto Him.

In response to Israel's question of how to return to Him, God offers tithes and offerings as a path of reconciliation. They are not ends unto themselves but a means to achieve God's purposes and will. Malachi's broader discussion emphasizes the breach in the relationship. The obedience and honor demonstrated through acceptable giving helps counteract the breach by drawing the giver into intimate fellowship with the Lord. The natural consequences of that fellowship are the blessings that flow from and through the relationship.

While the conclusions I've drawn required some interpretation of the scriptural text, the message from the second reference scripture is a bit more straightforward.

Hosea 6:6 (NKJV)
[6] *For I desire mercy and not sacrifice, And the knowledge of God more than burnt offerings.*

This passage sends a very simple message that God is more interested in our relationship with Him than our offerings. The "knowledge of God" is the essence of our salvation. It is the foundation of both the personal relationship God seeks to reestablish with us and our fulfillment of the first and greatest commandment. Jesus helps us to understand the meaning of this passage in Hosea when He defines the meaning of eternal life in John 17:1–3. Eternal life is our growing in our knowledge of God the Father and Jesus His son.

Malachi wanted us to see that God gives tithes and offering as a process to help heal our relationship with the Father. However, Hosea wanted us to understand that God desires to give of Himself to us more than He desires the stuff of our offerings. Finally, John clarifies for us that Jesus came that we might have life (John 10:10) and this is that life, that we may know God, and Jesus Christ whom He sent (John 17:3). This is the desire about which Hosea was speaking. God's priority was and is our relationship with Him. Jesus came that we might enter into a personal relationship with God, a relationship that we can pursue through our giving, but is more important than the gift itself.

God's Interest in
---
the Giver's Relationship with Others

Food for Thought
It is interesting to note that God often assesses our giving by first assessing the condition of our human relationships. While we focus on our gift, He chooses to examine how we are treating one another. Even the earliest scriptural account of giving (the story of Cain and Abel) speaks not only to the issue of the acceptability of Cain's offering, but also to issues involving Cain's relationship with God and Cain's relationship with Abel. How revealing it is that in a story about giving, Cain asks the eternal question, "Am I my brother's keeper?" The fact is that while we may desire for our giving to be viewed and judged as an independent spiritual activity, God refuses to do so and He purposefully keeps Cain's question ever before us even while we give.

Read the Following Reference Scriptures
Isaiah 1:10–17
Matthew 23:23
Matthew 5:23–24

Connecting the Dots:
What God has allowed me to see

In the third chapter of Malachi, God expresses displeasure with Israel's lack of giving tithes and offerings. In contrast, the reference scripture from Isaiah expresses God's displeasure in spite of Israel's giving. God's displeasure is not directed at the content of the gifts, but rather the context of Israel's behavior in which the gifts were offered.

The symbols and rituals of worship were present and yet God described the activity as meaningless, detestable and a burden. Something was missing. If the Israelites were like us, they probably saw little connection between the acceptability of their worship and giving and the condition of their human relationships. God asked for offerings and Israel gave the required offerings. They sought to comply with the ordinances and rituals of worship, yet God was not satisfied. As the prophet Isaiah described God's response to the activity of Israel's worship, I'm sure perplexed givers wondered: *What does God want from me? What does He want me to do?*

In God's response to these implied questions, it is important to note that God did not instruct Israel to alter its giving practices. Instead, God connected the acceptability of their giving to their activity in other areas. The common trait in the changes God sought in Israel was centered in the righteousness of their dealings with each other and, in particular, their dealings with the less fortunate in their society. God called for justice. Justice satisfies our need and expectation for fairness in our human relationships, but God also called for Israel to extend itself beyond the minimum requirements of legalism. His call for encouraging the oppressed, defending the cause of the fatherless and pleading the case of the widow reflected attributes of grace. The giver of grace extends beyond the bounds of what is required or deserved and offers that which blesses another. God extends more than justice to us; He gives His unmerited favor, His grace.

Jesus continues to convey the Father's heart on this matter in Matthew 23, which (like the passage in Isaiah) challenges ritualism that is devoid of righteousness in human dealings. In Matthew 23:23, Jesus comments on the detailed lengths to which the Pharisees would go to comply with the requirements of tithing. The Pharisees would tithe not just of their increase in crops and livestock, but even of the quantity of spices that they accumulated. While commending that the tithe should indeed be continued, Jesus condemns the fact that the more important matters of the law were being neglected. Among the things He noted as more important than their giving were the application of justice and mercy.

Again we see justice mentioned as a basic requirement and then the challenge to go beyond what is required. Jesus called for the application of mercy. While justice makes certain that the punishment does not exceed the crime, mercy judges that sometimes lessening the punishment or withholding it altogether achieves a greater benefit. These are gifts that God extends toward us with the full expectation that we also extend them to each other.

In Matthew 5, Jesus continues the theme of tying the acceptability of our giving with our conduct in our human relationships. Here, Jesus communicates that human relationship issues are not only important but urgent. How we conduct ourselves in our human relationships is of such a priority that Jesus urges givers to leave their offerings at the altar and to first pursue reconciliation with those they knowingly have offended. Reconciliation is an essential element of the work that Christ has done for us, but He not only desires that we would be reconciled to the Father, we must also be reconciled to one another.

These scriptures make it clear that by themselves our offertory gifts are simply not enough to please God. God wants more. When we give offertory gifts, we are giving from the material provision that we have received from God.

However, spiritually we have also received the gifts of God's grace, mercy and reconciliation. In addition to our offertory gifts, God also desires that we would give in our relationships with others that which we have received spiritually in our relationship with Him. In Matthew 10:8, as Jesus is sending His disciples forth to minister, He challenged them to freely give to others of the spiritual substance that they had freely received from Him. When we fail to give of our spiritual substance in addition to our material substance, God views our giving as incomplete.

God's Interest in

More than the Giver's Hand

Food for Thought

God is spirit. He has no temporal needs. God is the creator, sustainer and owner of all things in heaven and in earth, visible and invisible. His ownership has not diminished with time. His wealth is immeasurable. Yet, He still asks for our gifts. What could God possibly be seeking from us?

Reference Scriptures
Psalms 24:1–3
Acts 17:24–28
1 Chronicles 29:13–17

Connecting the Dots:
What God has allowed me to see

Psalms 24 emphatically declares that the earth is the Lord's. His sovereign authority over the world was established in power with the act of creation itself. It brings to mind the first chapter of Colossians where Paul summarizes that the world was created by God's power through the Son and for the Son and that by the Son He holds it all together. The Godhead alone spoke into existence that which is seen and unseen, the known and unknown. God did so without our help. Man was not a part of the creative process. Instead, we are the crowning product of the creation. The creation was and is God's possession. Everything in it belongs to Him. We can neither add to nor subtract from the wealth of His possession. As Paul reminded Timothy, we bring nothing into this world and we can take nothing with us when we leave (1 Timothy 6:7).

In the reference scripture in Acts 17, Paul's message to the Athenians helps us to understand, that as the creator of all things, God does not "need" gifts from our hands. Instead, it is He who gives us everything. As the owner of everything, God does not call us to give that He might gain. The money we give and churches we build have no impact on His financial standing. They do not increase His possession. Considering our giving in this context may help us realize that we often view our giving from a different perspective than God. Many of us approach our giving with the intent to help God and His work. Yes, God does invite our gifts, but with a different purpose in mind. While we are trying to do something for God (as an act of service), He is simultaneously working to do something (not just for us), but in us.

God is served not so much by what we do for Him, but by how our heart responds to Him.

When I search for the essence of Paul's message in the reference scripture, I come away with this: God is not seeking the product of our hand, He is seeking the response of our heart.

I think this principle is wonderfully illustrated in the biblical account of the offering that David and Israel gave for the building of the temple. Once again I refer to the passage in the twenty-ninth chapter of 1 Chronicles. However, this time my focus is directed at David's prayer. David possessed a passion to build a house of worship for the Lord. When David found it was not God's will that he be the actual builder of the temple, David chose to make advance preparation so that his son (Solomon) could complete the work. David gave a substantial offering to finance the construction of the temple. The people responded to David's example by giving a substantial offering of their own. David then praised God with the following prayer:

1 Chronicles 29:
1Ch 29:13 Now, our God, we give you thanks, and praise your glorious name.
1Ch 29:14 "But who am I, and who are my people, that we should be able to give as generously as this? Everything comes from you, and we have given you only what comes from your hand.

1Ch 29:15 We are aliens and strangers in your sight, as were all our forefathers. Our days on earth are like a shadow, without hope.

1Ch 29:16 O LORD our God, as for all this abundance that we have provided for building you a temple for your Holy Name, it comes from your hand, and all of it belongs to you.

1Ch 29:17 I know, my God, that you test the heart and are pleased with integrity. All these things have I given willingly and with honest intent. And now I have seen with joy how willingly your people who are here have given to you.

After considering his giving from the perspective we have discussed, David concluded that God uses the process of giving to test the integrity of our hearts. The gift of our hand is a gift of stewardship. As David says, through the gifts of our hands we simply return what belongs to God back to Him. However, it is in the response of our hearts that God finds pleasure. For our heart's response is our possession to give or withhold from God as we choose. This, more than the material substance of our gifts, is what God seeks. God wants more than a gift from our hand.

God's Interest in
————
the Giver's Faith

Food for Thought

There is a big difference between talking about faith and applying it. If God gave college classes in faith, they would be entitled "Applied Faith" rather than "Faith Theory." God wants faith working in every aspect of our relationship, even in our giving. As Hebrews 11:6 reminds us, "Without faith it is impossible to please God, because anyone who comes to Him must believe that He exists and that He rewards those who earnestly seek Him."

Reference Scripture

1 Kings 17:7–24

Connecting the Dots:
What God has allowed me to see

When I consider the biblical account of Elijah and the widow, I am struck first by the lengths to which God will go to increase the faith of individual believers. Secondly, I can't help but notice what an integral part giving can play in this process.

In order to understand what I've received from this passage, it helps to realize that this portion of the story is not about God's plan to feed Elijah in the midst of the drought. In the first seven verses of this chapter, God demonstrates His ability to feed Elijah by having ravens bring Elijah bread and meat daily. Ravens are not domesticated carrier pigeons. They are scavengers, selfish and self-centered, so God had them operate contrary to their nature to fulfill His will for Elijah. However, after establishing His care for Elijah's temporal needs, God moves the focus of the chapter to the spiritual needs of the widow. God chooses to minister to the spiritual needs of the widow through her giving.

God instructed the widow to give an offering of food to Elijah before his actual arrival. Though Elijah was sent to receive this gift from the widow, God's focus was on much more than the substance of her gift. In fact, all she initially had to offer was flour and oil. Elijah arrived and restated God's instructions and promises, but precedes them with a wonderful word of encouragement: "Don't be afraid." It has been said that our fear is simply misapplied faith. The word fear is sometimes an acronym for *f*alse *e*vidence *a*ppearing *r*eal, but God wanted to redirect the widow's faith from the appearance of her circumstances to Him, the Lord of our circumstances.

The widow redirected her focus from the fear of starvation to God's promises to sustain her. In response to her obedience, Elijah continued to stay with the widow. As she gave to Elijah, day by day God replenished her provision, but the best was yet to come. Later her son became ill and died and Elijah prayed to God on his behalf. God honored Elijah's prayer and restored the son's life.

God had not simply requested that the widow give, but that she give out of her lack. God had required that she give out of faith. He then used her faith to extend her provision, then the life of her son and finally the magnitude of her faith itself. I know that her faith was increased because she ends this biblical account with the declaration that she was now convinced that the words of the Lord from Elijah's mouth were the truth.

Even though we are willing to give, sometimes we are afraid to give when our resources are low or when the demands on our resources from creditors and other obligations seem high. Sometimes it seems difficult to give in faith, but Elijah's words of encouragement still bring comfort today—"Don't be afraid." When we realize that God gave the widow far more than He asked the widow to give to Elijah, it becomes easier to see that God was focused on more than just the widow's gift. God wanted to bless her, but there are certain blessings that are only released through the application of our faith. God wants to bless you too, but you have to be willing to do more than just give. Be willing to give in faith.

The Gift Is Still Important Because of What It Reveals

Sell your possessions and give to the poor. Provide purses for yourselves that will not wear out, a treasure in heaven that will never fail.... For where your treasure is, there your heart will be also.

— Luke 12:33 & 34 (TNIV)

OUR GIVING REVEALS
––––
THE GIVER'S LOVE

Food for Thought

It was February of 1999. For several months, I had shared a series of instructional thoughts on giving with my local church congregation just prior to the collection of the offering during Sunday worship service. As I sought the Lord for guidance concerning what to share for the upcoming Sunday, I was drawn to the spiritual symbolism embedded in our Valentine's Day tradition. A clear and simple principle emerged. Love gives.

Reference Scripture

John 3:16

Connecting the Dots:
What God has allowed me to see

During the Valentine season, millions of people anxiously wait to see what expressions of love they will receive. Some look for a tangible sign that the words of affection that they have heard expressed are in fact real. Others try to gauge the intensity of the romantic feelings of the potential gift giver, their level of commitment to the existing relationship or whether the "fire is still burning."

Some givers select and give gifts with much thought and reflection on the gift's appropriateness and the message it conveys. Others (out of ritual) make last-minute purchases from whatever is available. Still others search painstakingly for that which meets some minimum standard of social acceptability. Some gifts are given with gladness, but others reluctantly. Some are given with great anticipation, but others as an afterthought. Some give gifts in response to peer pressure. Some give nothing at all (confident that the potential recipient knows that they care).

One profound difference between the Valentine's Day ritual and our offertory giving is that God needs neither a designated event nor any artificial barometer to discern the state of our love for Him. He already knows. However, designated times of offering do present to us a mirror in which we get to see a glimpse of the state of our love for Him and the state of our relationship with Him. Many of us don't like what we see, so we refuse to look too closely. Some refuse to look at all, but the mirror is there just the same.

Setting aside for a moment all of the instruction in scripture about giving, we see that the scripture clearly demonstrates the love of the Father and the Son.

Acknowledgment of this love is among the most basic of Christian principles, and giving is the most fundamental expression of that love. The scripture is bursting with examples: God loved the world so much that He *gave* His Son (John 3:16). Jesus loved us so much that He *gave* His life (Matthew 20:28). Jesus stated that man's greatest love is expressed in his willingness to *give* his life for his friends (John 15:13). Paul commands husbands to love their wives as Christ loved the church and *gave* Himself for her (Ephesians 5:25). Paul comforts us with the thought that if God was willing to *give* His Son for us, how can He not be willing to also *give* us all things (Romans 8:32).

One January (a few years ago), my eldest son was home for a visit prior to transferring to the east coast for a new job. During a man-to-man/father-son chat, he advised me that he had a new female friend. I didn't ask him to categorize his level of emotional attraction, but listened intently to his description of his response to the developing relationship. He shared that his new friend was born in another country and how he had researched the national flower of that country and (as a spontaneous gift) had that single-stemmed flower delivered to her office by a florist. Then he shared how he planned to invite her to the grand opening of a play in Philadelphia, written and produced by one of his personal friends. I pondered how things would develop but didn't want to probe too deeply. I chose to simply observe over time how the relationship evolved. Early in February, he and I were in another conversation, this time discussing the More Than The Gift workbook. My son served as one of the workbook's beta readers, providing feedback concerning my message and method. He had just read the chapter entitled "A Love Problem" and commented that it was ironic that Valentine's Day was rapidly approaching. I took the opportunity to inquire about his Valentine's Day plans for his new friend. He replied that he wasn't sure whether he would buy her a gift. I thought for a moment about what he had just shared in the context of the message of the workbook's chapter. I paused and then advised him that his attitude and approach regarding this opportunity to give said volumes about the state of their relationship. In January there was an intention to please that manifested itself through spontaneous and creative expressions of giving. Yet, in February there were uncertain intentions and a hesitancy regarding any expression of giving at all. January spoke to a fervor of affection that seemed missing in February. Whether he was ready to admit it or not, something had changed and he would be well served to reflect on the message his feelings about giving a Valentine's Day gift revealed. The issue wasn't whether he ultimately gave a gift, but he needed to examine what his inner attitude and approach revealed about the true state of the relationship. The opportunity to give simply presented a vehicle for reflection.

God's relationship with us is a love affair. God (by example) demonstrates how intricately intertwined loving and giving are. God expresses His love by offering us His very best. "For God so loved the world that he gave…" However, the demonstration of love is not intended to be one-sided. As my son discovered, our opportunities to give present to us mirrors that reflect the condition of the underlying relationship. Mirrors are wonderful tools for self-examination. For those open to self-reflection, our attitudes and giving practices reveal telling signs of the health of our relationship with the Lord. Mirrors do not create reality, they simply reflect it. Our responses to our opportunities to give simply reflect the love condition that already exists.

Our Giving Reveals
----
the Giver's Gratitude

Food for Thought

Ten lepers stood by the side of the road, at a distance, calling in a loud voice to Jesus for mercy and grace. Ten lepers demonstrated their faith by following Jesus' instruction that they behave as if they were healed even before their healing visibly manifested itself. Ten lepers received a miracle and yet only one returned to acknowledge his healing. Only one threw himself at Jesus' feet. Only one used his loud voice to render praise and thanksgiving. Seeing this, Jesus asked His disciples, *"Were not all ten cleansed? Where are the other nine?"* (Luke 17:17) This biblical story reminds me that each day, each one of us should consider whether we are more like the one or more like the nine?

Reference Scriptures
Luke 19:1–10
John 12:1–8

Connecting the Dots:
What God has allowed me to see
In Luke 19, we are told the story of Zacchaeus' encounter with Jesus. Given his position as chief

tax collector, Zacchaeus was held in disdain by his fellow Jews. He both assisted the Roman government in their oppression of his people and then added to the oppression by forcing the people to pay higher taxes than actually required. Zacchaeus was a social outcast, yet Jesus extends to him both acceptance and redemption. Jesus extended His mercy and grace to Zacchaeus without being asked, for He knew Zacchaeus' need. What a gift! In response to Jesus, Zacchaeus offers to give half his wealth to the poor and repay fourfold to all he had cheated. What a response! Zacchaeus chose to demonstrate his gratitude in a visible way. His response served not only as a personal statement of thanksgiving, but also as a public testimony to the Lord's goodness.

In the second reference scripture, we see an example of gratitude that motivates offerings of more than just the giver's physical possessions. A dinner was held in Jesus' honor in Bethany, the hometown of Lazarus and his sisters Mary and Martha. Mary took an expensive perfume and anointed Jesus. It is clear in the scriptures that Mary was a worshiper of Jesus. During an earlier visit to Martha's home by Jesus (Luke 10:38–42), we find Mary sitting at Jesus' feet and listening to His every word. Martha questions Mary's actions, but Jesus commends them.

Luke 10:41 & 42

^{Lk 10:41} *"Martha, Martha,"* the Lord answered, *"you are worried and upset about many things,* ^{Lk 10:42} *but only one thing is needed. Mary has chosen what is better, and it will not be taken away from her."*

In the passage from the twelfth chapter of John, Mary's worship takes the form of an offering, an offering of great value. The perfume was worth about a year's wage. Why did she give such a gift? Jesus comments later (John 12:7) that the anointing served as preparation for His crucifixion and burial. While He knew this to be true, Mary was not aware of those coming events, so maybe her motivation was a little different, more personal. While Mary's motive is not actually stated, I believe it is implied. Mary's gift was an offering of thanksgiving, a response of gratitude for Jesus' amazing act of grace.

Mary's family had experienced more than Jesus' healing power. They had tasted of His resurrection power. Jesus had not simply healed their sick brother, but had revived him after he had been dead for four days and was in the grave. Through Jesus' actions they experienced levels of joy and faith they had not known before. This was not an accident, for it had been Jesus' intent to use Lazarus's illness to deepen His relationship with His followers by deepening their faith. Listen to His words to His disciples when discussing Lazarus prior to going to Bethany to perform the miracle of Lazarus' resurrection:

John 11:14 (KJV)
Jn 11:14 So then he told them plainly, *"Lazarus is dead,*
Jn 11:15 *and for your sake I am glad I was not there, so that you may believe, but let us go to him."*

What could be withheld from Jesus in light of what He had given? Was there anything too costly to give? Mary chose to withhold nothing. Some theologians believe that the perfume was contained in an alabaster box that once broken open could not be resealed. Once opened, if not used, the perfume would spoil. Therefore, to offer any to Jesus was to offer it all. Yet, we see that Mary offered not only the expensive perfume but herself as well. In Luke 10, we see Mary the worshiper, but not Mary the servant. Martha had been the one to offer service and complained that Mary would not help. Now we see Mary offering service as well, choosing not only to give the gift of the perfume but also to anoint Jesus herself and to wipe His feet with her hair. Her gratitude had expanded her willingness to give. Look at the progression of her relationship. First she gave worship, then she gave of her possessions and finally she gave of herself.

God's grace extends to us gifts of blessings and favor that we do not deserve. When we truly understand the great grace we have received from our Lord, it is natural to be overwhelmed with gratitude. When Mary and Zacchaeus experienced the Lord's grace, their gratitude motivated them to give. The witness of their giving revealed the gratefulness of their heart. In each case, more than the substance of what was given, their gifts had added importance from being a witness of their thanksgiving. Their giving was important because of what it showed.

OUR GIVING REVEALS

THE GIVER'S UNDERSTANDING OF GOD'S OWNERSHIP

Food for Thought

…As the king was walking on the roof of the royal palace of Babylon, he said, "Is not this the great Babylon I have built as the royal residence, by my mighty power and for the glory of my majesty?" The words were still on his lips when a voice came from heaven, "This is what is decreed for you, King Nebuchadnezzar: Your royal authority has been taken from you. You will be driven away from people and will live with the wild animals; you will eat grass like cattle. Seven times will pass by for you until you acknowledge that the Most High is sovereign over the kingdoms of men and gives them to anyone he wishes." Immediately what had been said about Nebuchadnezzar was fulfilled. He was driven away from people and ate grass like cattle. His body was drenched with the dew of heaven until his hair grew like the feathers of an eagle and his nails like the claws of a bird. At the end of that time, I, Nebuchadnezzar, raised my eyes toward heaven, and my sanity was restored. Then I praised the Most High; I honored and glorified him who lives forever. His dominion is an eternal dominion; his kingdom endures from generation to generation. (Daniel 4:29–34)

Genesis records that God entrusted mankind with stewardship of the earth. The trap that mankind falls into over and over again is that we (like Nebuchadnezzar) confuse stewardship with ownership. Whatever dominion God allows us to experience represents delegated authority, not a transfer of title. That which we seemingly obtained through our efforts still belongs to God. Failing to reconcile the issue of true ownership leads to confusion in our relationship with the Lord and our response to Him. When we fail to acknowledge God's ownership, we tend to behave like we are out of our minds.

Reference Scriptures
Acts 17:24 and 25
1 Chronicles 29:13–15

Connecting the Dots:
What God has allowed me to see
While in Athens, Paul tried to clarify for local philosophers the proper perspective on giving to the living God whom he served. Like many of us, they were confused about God's purposes in the process of giving. They attempted to appease their gods with temples and statues erected in

their honor, but Paul let them and us know that God is ultimately the creator of all things, the owner of all things and the giver of all things. He does not "need" anything from us because it is all already His. Instead, it is He who gives to us.

The American Association of Christian Counselors sponsors a certificate program in counseling entitled Caring for People God's Way. In it, Dr. Chris Thurman shares a wonderful story by Pastor Chuck Swindoll to illustrate the conflict and confusion that can arise when one holds an incorrect view regarding ownership. The story goes something like this. A woman enters the airport at the end of a long, tiring business trip. Like many other travelers, she stops by one of the airport stores, buys a magazine to read and a bag of cookies to munch, and then plops herself into a nearby chair to await boarding. After letting her thoughts wander over the events of the trip, she finally allows her mind to find refuge in the pages of her favorite magazine. Remembering the cookies, she reaches into the open bag on the table next to her and begins to enjoy her snack. A few pages into the article she's been reading, she notices the rustling sound of the cookie bag and, to her astonishment, sees the hand of the man sitting next to her extracting a cookie. This was not someone she knew. She is stunned and speechless. Maybe he thought she didn't notice. Seeking to reestablish her territorial rights, she quickly reaches for another cookie, making certain that the bag crinkles as loudly as possible, and settles back into her reading. After a few moments, she again hears the sound of her neighbor's hand entering and exiting the bag. The anger grows within her. She doesn't want to make a scene, they are just cookies, but they are *her* cookies and there is a sense of violation just the same. The scene repeats itself a few more times until there is but one cookie left in the bag. To her shock, the man takes the last cookie, breaks it in half, gently pushes one half toward her, pops the remaining segment in his mouth then gets up and walks away. Rage is now boiling within her. He certainly had no right to the cookies. His arrogance was infuriating. Where was the gratitude? What should she do? Should she go after him and demand reimbursement? As she stands to voice her protest, the steward announces over the intercom that her flight is ready for boarding and passengers in her section should come to the gateway. The interruption gave her a momentary distraction. With the announcement, she instinctively reaches into her shoulder bag to make certain her ticket and boarding pass are secure. Still watching the man walk away, as she feels for the ticket, she again hears the crinkling sound of a cellophane bag. *Oh no!* Glancing into the shoulder bag, there, next to her boarding pass, she sees her unopened bag of cookies. Washed with embarrassment, she realizes the grace of her departed neighbor—for now she finally comprehends that the bag of cookies on the table had not been hers, but his.[1]

The simple difference in her perspective regarding ownership made all the difference regarding her attitude. Having a proper perspective regarding the material possessions God allows us to enjoy impacts not only the attitude with which we receive but also the attitude with which we give to God.

Our second reference scripture records the prayer that King David offered after he and the people gave a substantial offering to support the building of the temple. Notice that David did not boast in his giving, but rather acknowledged that all of the abundance that they gave was actually from God's hand and belonged to Him. Out of a proper perspective, David gave praise and thanks for the privilege to give abundantly.

Reflecting on God's ownership liberates us from much of our internal turmoil regarding the giving of ourselves and the material substance in our possession. It should be calming, comforting and almost embarrassing to realize that we are the recipients of God's amazing grace (both spiritually and materially), a grace that often goes unperceived and unappreciated.

Consider for a moment the spiritual truth that you own nothing.

- It is God's bag ("the earth is the Lord's")

- They are His cookies ("and everything in it, the world, and all who live in it")

- God is the one that is sharing with you.

While Paul clarified that God does not actually need our gifts, David understood and clarified that our gift is still important because of what it shows. David illustrated that our attitude regarding giving to God reveals whether we understand who actually owns the substance that we give.

Our Giving Reveals
the Giver's Stewarship

Food for Thought

In the sixteenth chapter of Luke, Jesus tells the parable of an unjust steward. He concludes the parable with these words: *"Whoever can be trusted with very little can also be trusted with much, and whoever is dishonest with very little will also be dishonest with much. So if you have not been trustworthy in handling worldly wealth, who will trust you with true riches? And if you have not been trustworthy with someone else's property, who will give you property of your own? No one can serve two masters. Either you will hate the one and love the other or you will be devoted to the one and despise the other. You cannot serve both God and money."* (Luke 16:10–13)

This parable begins with a master telling his unjust servant that the servant must give an account of his stewardship. Jesus' words are clear. The faithfulness with which we handle God's resources reveals the focus of our stewardship. As was the case with that servant, a day of reckoning will come for each of us. On that day, our deeds will declare our allegiance and answer Jesus' implied question: Whose steward are you?

Reference Scripture
Mark 12:1–12

Connecting the Dots:
What God has allowed me to see

For our relationship with the Lord to develop properly, it is critical that we both understand and embrace our roles and responsibilities within the relationship. Understanding is an intellectual action. We can understand but choose not to act in accordance with that understanding. Embracing requires a voluntary commitment of our actions based on our understanding. For some, our struggle concerning the control of the resources we possess is more profound than a simple misunderstanding regarding God's ownership. Daily, each Christian faces choices between being spirit-led or self-directed. Self-centered choices are justified based on their convenience or satisfaction of our personal preferences and desires rather than their spiritual correctness. Whether subtle or overt in its expression, pursuit of self-directedness by a Christian reflects rebellion against God's lordship, against His ownership, and undermines our relationship with Him.

The human choice to ignore the rights of legitimate ownership is fairly common. The overt expression can be readily seen in the prevalence of theft in society. However, a more subtle expression can be seen in our attitudes toward the possession of property. In the absence of the visible presence of the real owner, people often develop a "squatter's mentality." Sometimes a borrowed item is in the borrower's possession so long that the borrower begins treating the item as if he or she owned it. Indeed, there are legal theories concerning "squatter's rights" whereby if someone is allowed to use another's property unchallenged for an extended period of time, the allowed use can evolve into a right of use. The squatter thereby assumes the privilege of ownership. We've all heard the expression that "possession is 9/10 of the law." This expression suggests the sentiment that the person in physical possession of an item is given the presumption of ownership. So in human dealings, we allow the assumption or presumption of ownership to be substituted for actual ownership.

This has spiritual implications because in the spiritual realm these human principles do not apply. Yet, we find our thinking on spiritual matters heavily influenced by how we operate in our human dealings. How do you view the things you have acquired in life? Whose are they really? Surely they were acquired by our effort, by the sweat of our brow. Yet, Paul asks, "… what do you have that you did not receive?" (1 Corinthians 4:7)

Choosing to hold a flawed perspective may lead to flawed actions, but it does not justify them. While the primary purpose of the parable in the reference scripture was to illustrate the attitudes of the religious leaders as respects their stewardship of God's people, there are also striking similarities to our attitudes toward giving offerings from the resources in our possession.

The violence of the vineyard managers was not the key point of the parable, but rather it was their willful disregard of the owner's instructions and their desire to keep the owner's goods for their own use and benefit. Many modern readers may have no familiarity with the sharecropping concepts of the parable, so let's use a more contemporary example. Most readers probably have some money in a bank or credit union. Even though that money is in the physical possession of the bank or credit union, everyone understands that the money actually belongs to the depositor. The bank or credit union serves as the steward of the money in its possession. Depositors allow the bank or credit union to use their money while it's in the institution's possession and both the depositor and the institution share in the profit made from such use. It is also understood that the depositor will periodically give the bank or credit union written instructions to distribute some funds to others. Those instructions are often in the form of a check, which directs the institution to pay a certain amount to the indicated payee.

Imagine your reaction if, in spite of the checks you issued for the payment of your bills, the bank or credit union:
1. decided to ignore your instructions and pay your creditors in accordance with their preferences because they decided that was a better use of your funds, or
2. couldn't pay the bills at all because they had used your funds to pay for the vacation of their employees.

Imagine your level of displeasure.

God has entrusted to us as stewards a portion of His possession. He fully intends that we benefit from our stewardship, but He also intends that portions of His possession would benefit the work and workers of ministry. He has given us some specific written instructions regarding the use of His possession, and sometimes He gives us additional instructions by the prompting of His Spirit. Each of us needs to examine our attitude toward offertory giving, for our attitude in giving reveals both our understanding and our acceptance of our role as God's steward. If we find ourselves altering the Lord's specific directions or ignoring His preferences, like the vineyard managers in the parable, we would do well to remember:

- It is the Lord's vineyard,

- They are His grapes, and

- He is the one that is sharing with us.

Our Giving Reveals
the Giver's Reverence

Food for Thought

Recently, I've been curious about the background of the Halloween tradition. Given its name, I've never quite understood what it was really about. The root word *hallow* means to make holy, to sanctify, to set apart for God. While the costumes, candy, dunking for apples and carving of pumpkins may be fun, our celebrations often do not make clear what (if anything) is being hallowed. My research revealed that the holiday itself is as confused as I was. It does not have a simple heritage, but evolved from the combination of a variety of Christian and non-Christian traditions. It contains a little bit of this and a little bit of that. I doubt that I am alone in my confusion. I suspect that many others also have no idea what they should be setting apart for God on that day. The emphasis of modern celebrations clearly reflects more of the non-Christian traditions, and because we have lost sight of or are unfamiliar with the intent, many of us fail to fulfill the godly purpose in the Christian portion of the tradition.

While I considered those thoughts, Deuteronomy 14:22 and 23 came to mind. This passage begins with an instruction that could easily be paraphrased—"Be sure to hallow a tithe of all you produce each year"—and the passage ends by explaining the purpose: "so that you may learn to revere the Lord your God always." Reflecting on this passage, I realized that our reverence for the Lord is enhanced as we hallow our offertory gifts to Him. As I think about offertory giving in our churches today, I wonder how often givers consider their gifts as holy, sanctified, specifically set apart for God. I wonder if our approach to giving helps us to learn to reverence the Lord. I wonder if, as with Halloween, many of us have lost sight of or are unfamiliar with the intent and therefore fail to fulfill God's intended purpose for our giving.

Reference Scripture
Malachi 1:6–14

Connecting the Dots:
What God has allowed me to see
Before we bring any offering to the Lord, it is critical that we prepare our hearts and minds. The object given is representative of the giver and the giver's heart. God is not so much interested in the gift. He is interested in you. In the reference scripture, God condemns the priests

and the people for lacking fear and reverence, for despising His name, for viewing His offering table as contemptible and for considering the offertory process "a burden." What an indictment!

The same concerns are valid today, maybe even more so. A respectful sense of awe and reverence is often lacking in our religious activity, including our giving. There is often casualness to our relationship with our Lord. Like the woman who anointed Jesus in the home of Simon the Pharisee, there should be occasions when we simply tremble and weep at the privilege of the presence of the Lord in our lives and the opportunity to give. There is a certain demeanor and behavior that parents expect from their children when in their presence. God asks, *"If I am a father, where is the honor due me?"* There is a certain restraint from misbehavior that employers expect from their employees in the presence of their managers. God asks, *"If I am a master, where is the respect due me?"*

Take an honest look at your own attitudes. Do you approach giving with a sense of awe and reverence? Does your giving honor the Lord's name or do you look upon the offering table with contempt? Has the act of giving become a "burden"?

While people may still be guilty of dishonoring attitudes, church leaders are also still guilty of passive acceptance. Silence on the part of church leaders makes them accomplices in the sin. Leaders cannot be afraid to confront the absence of reverence and let the people know that such attitudes are not acceptable to God.

How would you feel if you received a gift from someone you knew had no genuine interest in pleasing you? How would you feel if you knew the giver was just giving the minimum requirement to fulfill their sense of obligation or that the giving was purely ceremonial?

Do you wonder how God feels? Read the reference scripture again.

The passion God has for the reverence due Him is also revealed in the first three commandments given to Moses. These commandments speak to the position that God desires in our lives and His jealous protection of that position. Jesus summarized those commandments by saying we should love the Lord our God with all of our heart, soul and mind. God will accept nothing less than the preeminence that is due Him.

In the reference passage, God directly connects Israel's giving practices with the reverence that is due His name. First, He establishes that He has no tolerance for dishonoring attitudes and offerings. Hear His words from verse 10: *"Oh, that one of you would shut the temple doors, so that you would not light useless fires on my altar! I am not pleased with you,"* says the LORD Almighty, *"and I will accept no offering from your hands."*

Secondly, He makes it clear that our giving was meant to bring honor to His name. Let's look at verse 11: *"My name will be great among the nations, from the rising to the setting of the sun. In every place incense and pure offerings will be brought to my name, because my name will be great among the nations,"* says the LORD Almighty.

This principle is repeated in verse 14, which reads: *"For I am a great king,"* says the LORD Almighty, *"and my name is to be feared among the nations."* Our giving simultaneously serves as a personal act of worship and a public testimony to our esteem for the Lord. God desires both.

The Lord's Prayer begins with the words "Our Father in heaven, hallowed be your name." Sometimes these words flow easily from our lips without our realizing that God desires not to just hear them spoken but to see them applied. If His name is to be hallowed, then we are the ones who are called to do so. The passage in Malachi helps us understand that as we hallow both our attitudes and our offertory gifts, we also hallow God's name. In God's eyes, how we give clearly reveals our reverence for Him or lack of it.

Our Giving Reveals
----
the Giver's Treasure and Heart

Food for Thought

The comedian Jack Benny frequently performed a skit in which he portrayed an individual who was a "penny pincher." In the skit, a thief approaches the individual, pulls out a gun and says, "Your money or your life." The individual doesn't respond immediately, prompting the anxious thief to ask, "Well, what will it be?" Giving a very puzzled look, the individual finally responds, "I'm thinking, I'm thinking." The answer seemed so ridiculous that it was comical, yet as we all know, truth is sometimes stranger than fiction.

God desires to give us eternal life. However, eternal life is not measured by the length of our existence. It is measured by the depth of our relationship with the Father and the Son (John 17:3). God offers us the opportunity to give that we might experience life in Him more abundantly. God is not a thief, but He knows that we cannot serve two masters. We cannot serve both God and money. When material accumulation takes an unhealthy position in our value systems, He often allows us to be confronted with that critical question of choice: "Your money or your life?" Sadly, when faced with that choice, many people respond, "I'm thinking."

Reference Scripture
Mark 10:17–22
Luke 12:22–34

Connecting the Dots:
What God has allowed me to see
In this reference scripture in Mark, a young man approached Jesus in search of eternal life. The question that he posed suggested that he both believed that it was real and desired to have it. The fact that he ran to Jesus and fell on his knees to ask his question even suggests that eternal life was a priority to him. He was a man who had much and, like many of us, seemed to pursue a dream of "having it all." However, as many of us have discovered, pursuing "it all" often creates conflicting goals that require you to choose between options. It is there, in the face of such conflict that our priorities must be clarified.

The reference scripture says that Jesus looked at the man, loved him and discerned what he lacked to achieve his goal. Jesus wasn't trying to cause problems. He was trying to help the man. The question was not "How much do you have?" but "Whom do you serve?" The question was: "Who is your master?" It was a matter of choices, a matter of priorities, a matter of allegiance. Something had to come first.

Eternal life cannot simply be one of the many things we choose. It must clearly be our most important choice. So, Jesus told the young man to sell what he had and give to the poor and he would have treasure in heaven. Jesus' focus was (and is) on the eternal more so than the temporal. Jesus knows that one of our failings is that we tend to put great value on things that have little eternal worth. So He encourages us to exchange our unstable earthly currency for spiritual currency that has eternal value.

Jesus wants us to know that in order to gain real treasure, we must be willing to give up some things. In being willing to give, we actually gain. In being willing to lose, we actually save. This is why He says: *"Whoever wants to be my disciple must deny themselves and take up their cross daily and follow me. For whoever wants to save their life will lose it, but whoever loses their life for me will save it. What good is it for you to gain the whole world and yet lose or forfeit your very self?"* (Luke 9:23–25) (TNIV)

In the second reference passage, someone wanting Jesus to arbitrate a dispute with his brother concerning an inheritance confronted Jesus. Jesus used the opportunity to teach about treasure and trust. First Jesus commented on how the average person is caught up in a faithless daily pursuit of things that God knows we need and fully intends to provide us. We demonstrate very little faith, very little trust. God's trustworthiness is demonstrated in nature all around us, yet we do not perceive that He possesses greater love and care for us than the flowers of the field or fowl of the air. So the Lord cries out, "Oh ye of little trust." Jesus explains that God wants to give to us and He will, but we need to put our trust in Him rather than things. Jesus finishes with a lesson on how to obtain eternal treasure. Rather than trying to accumulate, we should give. His call for us to give is a challenge that helps clarify where our trust really lies.

Trust is the basic building block of a healthy relationship. Hebrews 11:6 states that without faith (trust) it is impossible to please God. Those that want a relationship with Him must not only believe that He exists, but they must also believe in His trustworthiness. As we begin to entrust God with our earthly treasure, we are also placing our hearts in His safekeeping. For where our treasure is, there is our heart also. God does not request that we give of our treasure that He might add to His wealth. God asks of our treasure because He is seeking our trust. He is seeking our heart and God knows that where we give our earthly treasures reveals the location of our heart.

The Gift Is Still Important Because of What It Accomplishes

This service that you perform is not only supplying the needs of the Lord's people but is also overflowing in many expressions of thanks to God. Because of the service by which you have proved yourselves, people will praise God for the obedience that accompanies your confession of the gospel of Christ, and for your generosity in sharing with them and with everyone else. And in their prayers for you their hearts will go out to you, because of the surpassing grace God has given you.

— 2 Corinthians 9:12–14 (TNIV)

What Our Giving Accomplishes:

God's Provision for His Ministry

Food for Thought

While the budget chairperson for my local church, I observed that many Christians struggle with the quantity of church funds that are expended for the compensation of church workers and benevolence ministries. For some, it seems easier for them to support the idea of ministry programs than to directly support the people who serve in ministry or are served by ministry. I am aware that many of us have grown more comfortable with models of church finances that are more dependent upon staff volunteerism than models that are based on fair staff compensation. I am also aware that those who are not recipients of benevolence may periodically question the prudence of the help extended to others. The support extended to the church staff members and the less fortunate is characterized by some as poor stewardship.

Yet the familiar scripture Malachi 3:10 still reads: *"Bring the whole tithe into the storehouse, that there may be food in my house...."*

I wonder how often we consider the practical intent of that statement. The food wasn't simply for ministry programs. It was for people. It was for the workers of ministry and the less fortunate. The model was designed by God. It reflected His original intent for the support of ministry efforts, and I believe it continues to be His intent today.

Reference Scriptures
Luke 10:1–9
Matthew 25:31–45
John 6:1–13

Connecting the Dots:
What God has allowed me to see
It is clear from each of these passages that Jesus expects the support of ministry to come from the church and that He considers ministering to the less fortunate as a ministry priority. The burden of support may seem impractical or even impossible, but Jesus spoke these words without repentance. Christians seek to shrink back from the task for different reasons. Some try to implement seemingly more practical models or supplements to God's plan. However, the practical is often not the path of God's leading to achieve His spiritual purposes. Others seek a theological release by questioning whether the Old Testament model of financial support for ministry is applicable to the New Testament church. However, our reference scriptures are the words of Jesus, not the words of Moses.

In the passage in Luke, Jesus instructed those He sent forth in ministry not to take any extra provision for themselves (neither purse, nor bag, nor extra sandals). They were to rely on the provision given by those to whom they ministered. The essence of Jesus' instructions is no different than God's Old Testament model.

When Israel entered into the "promised land," all of the tribes were given a portion of land as an inheritance except the tribe of Levi. The tribe of Levi was composed of the priests and all the other workers of ministry. The tribe of Levi was not given any land of their own to earn their provision. God made the tribe of Levi totally dependent on the various offerings that Israel gave to Him. This was not their request, it was God's plan.

Numbers 18:8–20 clarifies that the offerings (not just the tithes) were also given to the Levites. Verses 8 and 11 call this gift "your regular share"; verse 19 says, "It is an everlasting covenant of salt before the Lord for both you and your offspring"; and verse 23 states, "This is a lasting ordinance for the generations to come." That doesn't sound like a temporary plan to me.

While the scripture in Numbers focuses on the first tithe, which provided exclusively for support of the workers of ministry, the scripture in Deuteronomy 26:12 and 14:28–29 speak of a tithe that was taken every third year. This tithe supplied provision for ministering to the tangible needs of the less fortunate. In Matthew 25:31–46, Jesus continued this principle by communicating His priority for our ministering to the less fortunate. He states that at His second coming He will commend and condemn those gathered before Him based on their response to the needs of the hungry, the naked, the homeless, the sick and those in prison. He characterizes our response to those in need as equating to our response to Him. Just as the offerings in the Old Testament were considered offerings to God, Jesus equates our ministry to the less fortunate as ministry unto Him.

The natural question we ask is this: How can we meet such a great need? The answer lies in following God's plan. A wonderful illustration is provided in the accounts of Jesus feeding the 5,000.

Jesus asks Philip the rhetorical question of how to feed the multitude. To Philip, meeting the need seemed an impossibility. The accounts of this event written by Matthew and Luke reveals that the disciples wanted to send the crowd away. The offering of a young boy's lunch seemed woefully insufficient and yet it was all that was needed.

Their apparent lack turned into abundance because of God's blessing.

When God's people give in accordance with His purposes and plan it accomplishes God's provision for ministry. Our gifts and God's blessing are all that are required to generate more than we have room to receive. We don't need to question the blessing, it has already been promised.

Malachi 3:10
"Bring the whole tithe into the storehouse, that there may be food in my house. Test me in this," says the LORD Almighty, "and see if I will not throw open the floodgates of heaven and pour out so much blessing that you will not have room enough for it."

Look at what God accomplished in ministry to the 5,000 through a simple uninhibited offering. In response to Jesus' call to "bring it to me," the young boy gave what was asked of him. The boy gave, God blessed and the ministry need was met. If we lack provision for ministry today, maybe it is because we fail to answer God's call that we bring to Him that which He asks of us.

What Our Giving Accomplishes:

Our Fellowship in Ministry

Food for Thought

Every now and then, I am reminded that our human experiences often convey spiritual messages. Not so long ago, as I was carrying a large box through our home, my youngest son stopped me and asked, "Daddy, can I help?" A part of me wanted to politely reject his offer. The item was awkward and heavy and his attempt at assistance would actually slow down the progress I could achieve alone. However, when I looked down into his eyes I realized the true significance of the moment. The task at hand immediately lost its importance and I turned my focus to my son. I told him to grab a corner of the box. I repositioned my grip to make certain that there was no more weight on his corner than he could bear. As he placed his tiny hands on the box, his eyes began to glisten. Together we completed the chore, but now with a greater sense of fulfillment and joy.

On the human level, God allowed me to see that there is a bond that grows out of our co-laboring together. My son's partnering with me in my activity gave us an opportunity to fellowship together. Our working together actually nurtured our growing together. On the spiritual level, God allowed me to see that my activity with the Lord has the same effect. It's not that God needs my help to carry the load or get the job done faster, but when God allows me to participate with Him, God is offering me an opportunity for fellowship. After I received this spiritual message, God then led me to consider the profound implications this revelation has for my giving. My giving is never meant to be a burden. God does all of the heavy lifting. He is just inviting me to come alongside His activity. When I extend my hands to help and I think about what God is really doing, like my son, my eyes begin to glisten with joy at the opportunity for fellowship through co-laboring with my Father.

Reference Scriptures
Acts 2:42–47
3 John 3–8

Connecting the Dots:
What God has allowed me to see
I recently found an article on the Internet by Pastor Bob Deffinbaugh (pastor/teacher and elder at Community Bible Chapel in Richardson, Texas) that shared a wonderful scriptural insight. He observed that in the Old Testament there were

numerous individual offerings. Each offering had a distinct (God-given) purpose and a set of rules attached to it regarding what could be offered and how it was to be offered. Each offering served to fulfill a unique component of God's purposes for Israel's giving. However, the contemporary church often misses that distinctive view. We tend to think of offerings as a collective lump and that composite view is less detailed in its revelation of what God is accomplishing through different facets of our giving.[1]

It is fitting that Pastor Deffinbaugh made this observation as a preface to his discussion of the Fellowship (Peace) Offering. I have to admit that until now, I have never thought about the intent of that offering. The third and seventh chapters of Leviticus detail the characteristics of this offering. Some theologians believe that this offering was intended to reflect an appreciation for one's state of right relationship or peace (that is, fellowship) with God. This offering was not made to obtain peace with God, but to celebrate it. Its distinctive characteristics included the fact that it was the only offering where a portion of the sacrifice was shared between God, the priests and the person making the offering. The offerer's share from the sacrificial animal was consumed in a meal. Pastor Deffinbaugh noted that given the size of the offering and the requirement that it be consumed within two days, offerers probably shared this meal with friends as well. This sharing of the offering and the state of peace and communion between God and the offerer each embodied the symbolism of fellowship.

The reference scripture in Acts describes the pattern of life of the early church at Jerusalem. I find that their distinctive practices reflect an amazing connection to the distinctive characteristic of the Fellowship Offering. These believers were of one heart and mind. They routinely sold their possessions and brought the proceeds as an offering to the disciples (Acts 4:33–35). Believers shared in this offering so that no one lacked physical necessities. On a daily basis they also gathered in each other's houses and shared meals together. It is clear that one of the defining attributes of that community was their fellowship. Acts 2:42 says they devoted themselves to "the fellowship." Their concept of fellowship involved more than the just being in each other's company and getting to know one another. The phrase "the fellowship" described more than what they did, it also described who they were. As the New Testament church grew, the language used to reflect their fellowship with each other and with God subtly expanded to reflect the breadth of their bond. New Testament writers referred to believers as fellow-citizens, fellow-heirs, fellow-prisoners, fellow-servants, fellow-soldiers and fellow-workers. It was the composite of these descriptions that defined the deep quality of their fellowship.

For the New Testament church, fellowship embodied more than their oneness in belief and social activity, but also a communion in labor. This co-labor included their giving. In both reference scriptures, we see their giving as a central component of their concept of fellowship. Their giving helped create a common experience, a shared experience, and allowed them to participate in the ministry labor of others.

In John's third epistle, he expresses his great joy for the hospitality extended by Gaius (an individual believer) to Christian missionaries that visited his area. Witness of his charity spread within the church. John encouraged Gaius to continue demonstrating generosity when the missionaries decided to leave. He noted that the missionaries had taken no financial support from nonbelievers and ought to be supported by other believers. John then observed that Gaius' gift of hospitality would make him a "fellow worker" in their ministry. Though his specific acts of benevolence are not stated in this passage, it is clear that John believed that Gaius' gifts bonded him in labor with these missionaries.

For New Testament believers, fellowship was essential both in supporting their ministry efforts to others and in the fulfillment of ministry's purpose within themselves. God's purposes for our fellowship have not changed over the ages. Hear Jesus' words as He prays for all believers of all ages

Jn 17:20 *"My prayer is not for them alone. I pray also for those who will believe in me through their message,*

Jn 17:21 *that all of them may be one, Father, just as you are in me and I am in you. May they also be in us so that the world may believe that you have sent me.*

Jn 17:22 *I have given them the glory that you gave me, that they may be one as we are one:*
Jn 17:23 *I in them and you in me. May they be brought to complete unity to let the world know that you sent me and have loved them even as you have loved me.*

Jesus said that the unity of believers with each other also bonds believers with God and witnesses to the unbelieving world. That unity is reflected in our fellowship and our giving is both an element and a symbol of that fellowship. As I considered this, I began to understand that God intends for our giving to simultaneously promote and embody the full breadth of our fellowship in ministry (our peace with God, our unity with other believers and our co-labor in the gospel).

What Our Giving Accomplishes:
Positions Us for Greater Blessing

Food for Thought

The Holy Scriptures are full of rich and wonderful promises for the believer. They are exciting to uncover and humbling to ponder. Each promise reveals the matchless nature of God's love for us and the benefits He wants us to experience through our relationship with Him. Some promises are simply our birthright, as we become daughters and sons of God through faith in Jesus Christ. Other promises are rewards or blessings that flow from our actions. In this spirit, God has ordained that abundant blessings flow from our giving. As a result, our giving actually positions us for greater blessings than we would otherwise experience. I am reminded of the Old Testament account of the widow from Zarephath. When Elijah met the widow, by her own admission, she and her family were positioned to die. Their circumstances had brought them to the point of starvation. Then God sent Elijah with a word of hope, but this word of promise was preceded by a request that the widow give from the very last of her provision. As she gave, she and her family were repositioned. Rather than being recipients of death, they became recipients of an increase in their food supply, an increase in health and an increase in faith. Greater blessings flowed from her giving than she ever imagined.

Reference Scriptures
2 Corinthians 9:6–8
Malachi 3:10–12
Luke 6:38
Proverbs 3:9 and 10

Connecting the Dots:
What God has allowed me to see
It is undeniable that abundant blessings flow specifically from the manner and magnitude of our giving. God responds to offerings that honor Him with great blessing. I remember an old offertory song from my childhood whose chorus contains the words, "You can't beat God's giving, no matter how you try. The more you give, the more He gives to you. Just keep on giving because it's really true that you can't beat God's giving, no matter how you try."[1] That is the essence of the reference scriptures. No matter which one you read, the message is the same. As you give to the Lord, He gives back in multiples. You will reap generously or He will open the floodgates of heaven and pour out blessings that you will not have room enough to receive or it shall be given unto you, good measure, pressed down, and shaken together and running over or

your barns will be full and your vats running over.

Make no mistake; the word of God is true. The blessings may occur on either a spiritual or material level, but if God has spoken it, He shall do it. If He has purposed it, it will surely come to pass (Isaiah 46:11). I believe that the children of God should live with an unwavering expectation of the promises of God and that our expectation should include the present, not just someday in heaven. As David said, "I would have lost heart, unless I had believed that I would see the goodness of the LORD in the land of the living" Psalm 27:13 (NKJV).

Giving does not create a lack in our provision. God simply wants to broaden our perspective to help us realize that He is our provision, our source, and in Him there is no lack. This is the God that inspired David to declare, "The Lord is my Shepherd, I shall not want…. My cup runneth over" (KJV). This is the God that sustained the flour and oil of the widow of Zarephath so that after feeding Elijah, her supply kept replenishing itself. This is the God that fed Israel for forty years in the wilderness with manna from heaven. This is the God that multiplied a boy's lunch of two fishes and five loaves of bread and fed 5,000 men (in addition to women and children).

Yet, as exciting as these principles are, there is a subtle risk of overemphasizing God's gifts to the detriment of the giver Himself. There is a danger that we'll focus on the "blessings" while neglecting the One from whom all blessings flow. Seeking to obtain the promises should not become the primary motivation for our behavior. Like the singer John P. Kee, I believe that it honors the Lord much more when we seek His face rather than just His hand. My desire is for us to honor God with our giving and then to see His blessings not as the goal, but as a natural consequence of giving that pleases Him. He must be the object of our attention and affection, not the things we can obtain from Him.

In Genesis 15:1, God tells Abraham, *"I am thy exceedingly great reward."* Whether God chooses to make our cup run over or simply makes certain that our cup never runs out, it really does not matter because He is our provision. He is our reward. Jesus knew that people have trouble drawing the subtle distinction and so in John 6, while debating with followers regarding the manna God gave Israel in the wilderness, Jesus declares unto them, "I am the bread that came down from heaven." In my mind I can hear Him saying, *Don't focus on the manna, focus on Me.*

Even though our giving positions us to be blessed, the greater blessing tends to be beyond the thing that we seek. In John 6:26, Jesus says, *"Very truly I tell you, you are looking for me, not because you saw the signs I performed, but because you ate the loaves and had your fill. Do not work for food that spoils, but for food that endures to eternal life, which the Son of Man will give you."* When the widow of Zarephath gave to the prophet Elijah, she did so in response to his promise that her provision of food would be sustained. Through her giving, she gained not only the fulfillment of that promise, but she also discovered the truth of God's word. Her biblical story ends with her declaring to Elijah: "…Now I know that you are a man of God and that the word of the Lord from your mouth is the truth" (1 Kings 17:24). What she received in return for her gift was not just food for her body, but food for her soul, food that endures to eternal life, the greater blessing!

What Our Giving Accomplishes:

Our Preparation for Eternity

Food for Thought

Best-selling author Randy Alcorn offers insight regarding how our handling of material possessions reveals the relative value we place on time and eternity. He portrays our lives as a line that begins with our birth and then extends endlessly from that point. He portrays time as a dot on that line. Given the insignificance of the dot when compared to the immeasurable length of the line, he suggests that a wise person should conduct his or her life in light of the line rather than the dot, in light of eternity rather than time.[1]

Two illustrations help clarify his point. Randy suggests that most of us would think it odd if during an airplane flight, a passenger placed expensive draperies over the windows, attached family photos to the seat in front of him or her and painted murals on the walls. Someone expending so much effort to get comfortable on an airplane would puzzle us because both the duration of the flight and their residence on the plane would be relatively brief.[2] It would seem a waste of resources to treat as permanent that which was clearly temporary.

Randy also asks you to imagine yourself as a northerner who lived in a southern state (that was part of the Confederacy) as the civil war was coming to an end and victory by the North was imminent. You had amassed great wealth in the South but planned to return to the North. Prudence would suggest that you convert as much confederate currency as possible to things that would be of value after the war ended, because at the war's end confederate currency would be worthless. So while a portion of your resources would continue to be used to sustain yourself, you would also urgently begin diverting resources in preparation for the transition.[3]

While most of us like to think that we behave rationally, I have concluded that many of us spend our time decorating airplane cabins while not preparing to ever leave the plane and go home. Many of us spend our lives accumulating things without considering that they soon will become worthless. Many of us exhaust our life's time and life's resources without ever preparing for our inevitable transition from time to eternity.

Reference Scriptures
Hebrews 11:8–10
1 Chronicles 29:13–17

Luke 12:29–34
Matthew 19:21

Connecting the Dots:
What God has allowed me to see

In recent years, the message from the passage from Hebrews has resonated within me with increasing strength. So many contemporary Christian messages focus on our reaping the benefits of God's promises and the blessings of our inheritance here on earth. This reference scripture presents the attitudes of our spiritual patriarchs in stark contrast to those sentiments. Abraham was the recipient of God's covenant promises. Part of that promise was he and his seed would inherit the land of Canaan. Yet, Abraham understood that his physical possession of Canaan was symbolic of the greater inheritance for which God was preparing him. Abraham kept his eye on the greater blessing yet to come. This scripture tells us that Abraham dwelt in the land of promise like a stranger in a foreign country and that he chose to live in tents rather than build a permanent residence because he was looking forward to another city whose builder is God. Abraham knew that his time in Canaan was temporary. Canaan was part of the promise, but Canaan was not his home. Abraham understood that he was a citizen of another kingdom.

This sentiment was not Abraham's alone. The scriptural passage shares that Abraham's son and grandson (Isaac and Jacob) who were heirs of the same promises, also chose to live in tents. The summary verses conclude by saying that Abraham, Sarah, Isaac and Jacob all acknowledged that they were strangers and exiles on the earth and that they were seeking a better country, a heavenly one. While they received some blessings on earth, they understood that the ultimate fulfillment of God's promises could not be received in this life. The fulfillment was yet to come. This life only offers a foreshadowing of the blessings God has prepared for us.

Often, I've found myself consumed by my focus on the next car, the next raise, the next promotion, the next home, or achieving a certain level of material comfort. Yet as I read the reference scripture, I remember the Lord asking the rich fool: "…when your soul is required of you, whose shall all these things be?" I hear Abraham whispering: *Don't set your sights so low. Don't sell your affections short. Set your focus on that which is dear rather than that which is near. Canaan is not your home.*

The reference scripture from Hebrews reveals a glimpse of how our spiritual patriarchs viewed themselves and how that impacted their handling of material possessions. The prayer by King

David in 1 Chronicles gives insight into God's perspective. In verse 15, David acknowledges that we are aliens and strangers in God's sight. However, I believe that God views us not as aliens and strangers to Himself, but rather as aliens and strangers on this earth. Our days on earth are like a shadow. They are fleeting. As the light of day dims, shadows fade and then vanish. Like a shadow, our existence on earth has no hope of permanence. What makes this passage particularly relevant is that David makes this observation in the context of a prayer to God regarding his giving. David knew that God uses our giving to test our hearts and David implies that our status as aliens and strangers on earth should impact how we respond to the test.

David and the leaders of Israel had given an offering for the building of God's temple. The magnitude of the offering was mind-boggling. David had personally given an offering of over 100 tons of gold and over 250 tons of silver. Israel's leaders then responded by giving an offering of even greater magnitude. In today's dollars, their combined offering was worth billions of dollars. It was immediately after thanking God for the privilege of being able to give in this manner that David shares the perspective that Israel and their forefathers were strangers and aliens on earth. David understood the same principle that Abraham understood and it is clear that David felt that this perspective facilitated their ability to give freely and generously to the work of God's kingdom.

In the reference scriptures in Luke and Mathew, Jesus contrasts our pursuit of the temporal with our pursuit of the eternal. The contrast is important because we are eternal beings who temporarily reside in mortal bodies. Our bodies are made of flesh and our flesh both needs and craves things, which like itself are temporal. However, the earthly things we crave don't last. They are subject to corruption and loss. Our flesh and all that it craves will soon pass away, but we will not.

We are eternal beings. So Jesus suggests that we shift our focus from the temporal to the eternal. The treasures in heaven do not share the frailties of earthly treasure. Therefore they represent a better investment of our time, energy and affection. The choice we make between investing in the temporal or investing in the eternal reveals the location of our heart. In our love relationship with the Father, He is always interested in the focus of our heart. However, a simple question emerges, how does one invest in the eternal?

In Luke 12, Jesus answers this question. Earlier in the chapter, He reminds us that life does not consist of the things we possess nor the food we eat nor the clothes we wear. In the reference scripture, He notes that God knows our need for these things. He knows that we are often consumed by our pursuit to obtain the things we need. Unfortunately, our pursuit of things minimizes our distinction from nonbelievers. So, Jesus reminds us that a believer's priority should be God's kingdom and He encourages us with the assurance that it pleases God to grant us citizenship in that kingdom.

Jesus then links our pursuit of the kingdom with our investment in the eternal. One way that investment is made is through our giving. In verses 33 and 34, He uses the same phraseology as in Matthew 6:20 and 21, which clarifies that our giving lays up treasure in heaven for us. This treasure awaits us in the same eternal country sought by Abraham, a kingdom whose builder is God. Our giving in the temporal world produces eternal treasure in the kingdom that is to come. As such, our giving represents more than a simple investment in the future because the future is a component of time and God's kingdom is not subject to time. Instead, through our giving we acknowledge our true citizenship and make preparation to go home. Through our giving, we make preparation for eternity.

WHAT OUR GIVING ACCOMPLISHES:

OUR PREPARATION FOR OUR INHERITANCE

Food for Thought

When our twin sons were infants, my wife and I researched investment options to save funds for their future. One very interesting option was a gift trust mutual fund. This investment had a remarkable performance record. It had increased in value by more than 20 percent for each of the preceding ten years. However, there was one characteristic of the investment that concerned us. It was an irrevocable trust, which required that any contributions we made become the permanent property of the trust for the benefit of our sons (as beneficiaries). We could put money in, but we couldn't decide later to take it out. At the predetermined time the trust would be available for our sons to use as they wished. We could not decide to withhold the funds if they made poor choices. That was a very scary thought because in spite of our love for our sons, we knew it was impossible to predict whether our infant sons would become wise stewards as adults. We had no desire to pre-fund unwise choices they might opt to make later. Prudence suggested that we invest the funds in a manner where we would retain control over their distribution. So, we chose not to commit substantial treasure to our sons' ownership prior to their developing and demonstrating the judgment to handle it. However, we simultaneously committed to using a weekly allowance to help them acquire and demonstrate that judgment. While their allowance was small, it seemed big to them. It gave them the opportunity to acquire basic skills for handling wealth by practicing with a small amount. Handling their allowance was a foundational step in preparation for incremental increases in responsibility and the eventual receipt of their inheritance. When I think about it, it becomes clear that God gives each of us opportunities for earthly stewardship to prepare us in very much the same way.

Reference Scriptures
Matthew 25:14–30
Luke 16:10–12
Matthew 25:31–40

Connecting the Dots:
What God has allowed me to see
After creating the world, God bestowed upon Adam and Eve the responsibility for stewardship of the earth. Since that time, humankind has seemed to continually struggle with its role as steward. I suspect that the inability of

contemporary Christians to understand "what's in it for me" contributes to our struggle. Many of us appear to share the attitude of the servant in the reference scripture in Matthew who was entrusted with one talent. That steward seemed to secretly fear that the owner wanted to receive a disproportionate share of the results of the steward's labor. So, the faithfulness with which he exercised his role was less than diligent. He bore the title of steward, but his heart appeared disconnected from the role.

In this reference scripture, Jesus says that we can learn spiritual lessons about His kingdom by considering the illustration He offers of an interaction between a property owner and his servants regarding their stewardship of his property. In Jesus' illustration, the owner gave responsibility to each steward based on the steward's individual ability. The owner's assessment of each steward's performance was based first on the faithfulness of the steward's effort rather than the magnitude of his productivity. The owner was pleased or displeased based on his assessment of their diligence. Faithful performance was rewarded with increased incremental responsibility. Faithful management of a little led to an opportunity to manage more. On the surface, it might appear that the owner was only serving his self-interest in order to increase his wealth until one considers the owner's invitation that the faithful stewards come share in his joy. The steward of the single talent did not comprehend that the owner fully intended that each steward's faithfulness would benefit the steward as well. Faithful stewardship was intended as an opportunity for blessing rather than a source of burden.

Drawing spiritual lessons from this illustration should begin to comfort those wondering "what's in it for them." Like the owner in the illustration, our Lord also will reward faithful stewardship. Like that owner, God seeks to enlarge the territory of our stewardship. Doing so brings Him joy, and, like the owner, He wants to share His joy with us. He carefully assigns our stewardship in light of our individual ability. God is looking for more than productivity from us. He is seeking faithfulness, but always has our mutual benefit in mind.

However, the Lord doesn't stop there. While Matthew 25 begins to open our understanding of the Lord's intent for our stewardship, I believe that Luke 16 adds important perspective to that understanding. The steward in Luke 16 was deemed unjust because he had handled the property given to his care more for his personal benefit than the benefit of the property's owner. In the reference verses, Jesus draws a spiritual parallel and explains that the consequences of such stewardship are to the detriment of the steward. A key to unlocking the spiritual implications of this message lies in first understanding that the implied "who" in Jesus' summary is God. I draw this conclusion because only God can give true riches that are greater than worldly wealth. Jesus wanted His listeners to understand that God doesn't simply desire to give us more of His property to manage, but He desires to give us property of our own that is of great value. Let me paraphrase verses 11 and 12 to highlight the interpretation I am suggesting:

God desires to give you true riches, but how can He trust you with true riches if you haven't been trustworthy in handling worldly wealth, which are not true riches. God doesn't want you to just manage His riches. He wants to give you riches of your own. However, how can He trust you to handle property of your own when you have not been trustworthy in handling His property?

I believe that God uses our roles as stewards as a tool of preparation. Like a parent, God gives us worldly wealth in amounts He considers of little value in order to train us how to manage the things of greater value He has prepared for us. Things He calls true riches. Like a parent, He assigns us the responsibility to care for portions of His property in order to prepare us for the day when we will become owners rather than just stewards.

So far, I have spoken about God's plan for our stewardship in general, but I have not mentioned any specifics regarding our stewardship in giving. The last reference scripture highlights this element of stewardship.

The setting involves the second coming of Christ. All nations are gathered before Him as He sits on His throne of glory. Jesus separates those who stand before Him based on how they ministered to others, based on how they gave of their possessions and of themselves. Listen to His words: "…when I was hungry you gave me something to eat, when I was thirsty you gave me something to drink…I needed clothes and you clothed me" (Matthew 25:35–36). Jesus is speaking specifically to stewardship in our giving. Christian stewardship is intended to embody more than taking care of the Lord's property. It involves putting it to productive use that can yield spiritual fruit. Faithful stewardship in giving achieves this goal by ministering to others on behalf of the kingdom. As we minister to the needs of others, we plant spiritual seeds in their lives from which God can reap a harvest. As we bless others, ultimately we bless the Lord Himself. Hear Jesus' response to those who had been faithful stewards in their giving: *"Come, you who are blessed by my Father; take your inheritance, the kingdom prepared for you since the creation of the world."* (Matthew 25:25–34)

When I consider all of the reference scriptures together, I realize that while our stewardship blesses God, His intent is that it help prepare us for blessings also. I realize that the benefit we receive is not simply a spontaneous reaction by God, but it reflects His intent for us, His plan for us since the dawn of creation. I realize that He is actively participating in our preparation and patiently awaiting our readiness to share in His joy, our readiness to take possession of true riches, our readiness to assume a position of ownership, our readiness to receive our inheritance. What's in it for me? Joy! True riches! Ownership! My inheritance! Wow!

WHAT OUR GIVING ACCOMPLISHES:
––––
BRINGING GLORY TO GOD

Food for Thought

Battles over which biblical principles should guide our giving can bog down discussions regarding Christian offertory giving. I think that much of the problem arises as we focus on scriptures in isolation rather than also trying to "connect the dots." I have purposefully chosen to illustrate the lessons in this book from both Old and New Testament scriptures. The messages that I have received flow from the harmony and wholeness of God's Word. God has not changed and He has been unveiling His purposes and plans for our giving since the time of Cain and Abel. Revelation of those purposes and plans are found throughout the Holy Scriptures, yet the church continues to struggle with interpretations of the messages and their appropriate application.

The lessons in this book offer glimpses of how God is leading me to "connect the dots." I find that the cord of relationship binds the messages together in the context of God's purposes and plans for our salvation. This connection flows from salvation's focus, our intimate relationship with our God. While I have tried to provide a harmonizing perspective through this lesson series, I have little doubt that differences of opinion will remain until Christ's return. I'm reminded of Paul's discussions of legalism and grace regarding the eating of meat that had been offered to idols. Paul knew that the insights he offered would not conclusively settle the debate. So, he concludes his discussion by saying, "Whatever you do, do all to the glory of God" (1 Corinthians 10:31). I can think of no sounder advice on which to base this last lesson. In Isaiah 43:7 we are told that God created those who are called by His name for His glory. I will conclude this lesson series by attempting to point us and our offerings toward that purpose.

Reference Scriptures
Malachi 1:10–14
2 Corinthians 9:7–14
Psalms 96:1–9

Connecting the Dots:
What God has allowed me to see

It is clear from this passage in Malachi that the Israelites had lost the passion of worship in their giving. They continued to engage in the ritual, but God was neither fooled nor pleased by their pretense. The attitudes of the people were marked by self-centeredness. It seems that their sole focus was on how offertory giving impacted them. They had lost their focus on God.

The Lord's focus is relationship-centered. It is through a healthy relationship that His name is glorified. Only when our offerings are God-focused can they help sustain health in the relationship. However, the book of Malachi speaks to the ill health of Israel's relationship with God. In the reference passage, the symptoms manifested themselves in how Israel approached their offerings to the Lord. So, God cries out in verse 6: "… if I am a father, where is the honor due me?" In verse 10, He makes it clear that though defiled gifts were being offered, He had no intention of accepting them. God's name was at stake and His name must be reverenced, even through our giving.

For much of my life, it seems that the Christian church has been singing the same old song regarding our giving. I am not speaking of our offertory music, but rather the teachings and practices regarding our giving. The song has a chorus that seems centered on us. It rings in our ears but has failed to inspire our hearts. It seems that many of us hum along as we go through ritualistic motions that lack the passion of real worship. It seems that many of us give for self-centered reasons or grudgingly or under compulsion, but Paul reminds us in 2 Corinthians 9:7 that this is exactly what God does not seek. Our situation reminds me of Israel in Malachi's day. It seems that they sang the same song we sing. It also reminds me of the church at Laodicea described in Revelations 3. That church was neither hot nor cold. Their lukewarmness nauseated God. It made Him want to vomit.

The reference passage in 2 Corinthians gives an illustration of what it would look like if we approached our offerings in a manner focused on God and His purposes. It's a glimpse of what it would be like if we began to sing a new song. The Christians in Jerusalem were being persecuted and were impoverished. Paul opened this passage with a prayer for the Corinthian Christians who would give to help meet the needs of the Jerusalem church. Paul speaks first regarding the enrichment that the givers would receive. However, he clarifies that the increase in prosperity was intended to position the givers to increase their generosity in giving. The primary benefit that flowed from the blessing of prosperity was meant to be enriched liberality. That enriched liberality would yield a multitude of fruit. The first fruit would be a response of thanksgiving for their generosity. In addition, their generosity would become a witness of both Paul's ministry and the givers' confession of the gospel. God would be glorified because of this and prayers would be offered on the givers' behalf.

Paul clearly had an expectation that the blessings of his prayer would be realized. Yet his song of expectation was very different from the self-focused refrains sung by many contemporary believers. Paul did not encourage the Corinthians to focus on themselves. He viewed the Corinthian church as neither the catalyst nor the primary object of the blessings. They were conduits of God's purposes. While the Corinthians served as sowers of seed, it was God who gave seed to the sower, multiplied the seed and enriched the sower. While the Corinthians would be enriched, it was so their generosity could benefit others. Others would see the witness of their liberality and give thanks, praise, prayer and glory to God. The Corinthians were participants in God's activity, but only through God's grace working in them. God initiated their giving for His purposes and for His glory.

Paul sang a different song regarding Christian giving and challenges us to sing a new song also. Consider the lyrics from Psalms 96.

Ps 96:1 **Sing to the LORD a new song; sing to the LORD, all the earth.**
Ps 96:2 **Sing to the LORD, praise his name; proclaim his salvation day after day.**

MORE THAN THE GIFT

Ps 96:3 Declare his glory among the nations, his marvelous deeds among all peoples.
Ps 96:4 For great is the LORD and most worthy of praise; he is to be feared above all gods.
Ps 96:5 For all the gods of the nations are idols, but the LORD made the heavens.
Ps 96:6 Splendor and majesty are before him; strength and glory are in his sanctuary.
Ps 96:7 Ascribe to the LORD, O families of nations, ascribe to the LORD glory and strength.
Ps 96:8 Ascribe to the LORD the glory due his name; bring an offering and come into his courts.
Ps 96:9 Worship the LORD in the splendor of his holiness; tremble before him, all the earth.

This song contains a message easily conveyed by our lips, but the psalmist challenges us to also convey it through our giving. The song's focus is centered on God and His activity. If we are to sing a new song, we need to realize that God's activity through us can sing more convincingly than our tongues. If we are to sing a new song, it is time for our offerings to sing praise to the Lord. It is time for our offerings to declare our salvation. It is time for our offerings to extend God's marvelous deeds among all peoples. It is time for our offerings to give worship to our Lord. It is time for our offerings to help us accomplish the purpose for which we were created: to declare

God's glory among the nations and render the glory due to the Lord's name. Amen!

NOTES

PROVIDING CONTEXT
1. Randy Alcorn, *Money Possessions and Eternity* (Wheaton, Illinois: Tyndale House Publishers, 2003), xii

2. Wesley Willmer, *Revolution in Generosity* (Chicago, Illinois: Moody Publishers, 2008), 26–27

GOD'S INTEREST IN THE GIVER'S UNDERSTANDING OF GOD'S OWNERSHIP
1. Dr. Chris Thurman, *Caring for People God's Way* (Forest, Virginia: American Association of Christian Counselors), BICO 104

WHAT OUR GIVING ACCOMPLISHES: OUR FELLOWSHIP IN MINISTRY
1. Pastor Bob Deffinbaugh, *The Fellowship Offering* (http://www.bible.org)

WHAT OUR GIVING ACCOMPLISHES: POSITIONS US FOR GREATER BLESSING
1. Caravans "You Can't Beat God's Giving." *You Can't Beat God's Giving*. Savoy, 1958

WHAT OUR GIVING ACCOMPLISHES: OUR PREPARATION FOR ETERNITY
1. Randy Alcorn, *The Treasure Principle* (Colorado Springs, Colorado: Multnomah Books, 2001), 50

2. Randy Alcorn, *Money Possessions and Eternity* (Wheaton, Illinois: Tyndale House Publishers, 2003), 102

3. Randy Alcorn, *The Treasure Principle* (Colorado Springs, Colorado: Multnomah Books, 2001), 13–15

Contact the author for more details:
morethanthegift@gmail.com
morethanthegift.com

www.ingramcontent.com/pod-product-compliance
Lightning Source LLC
Chambersburg PA
CBHW020009050426
42450CB00005B/390